In case of loss, please return to:

_____

_____

_____

_____

As a reward: $_____

CREATION RESTORED

THE GOSPEL ACCORDING TO GENESIS

MATT CARTER
& HALIM SUH

Published by LifeWay Press®
© 2012 The Austin Stone Community Church

ISBN: 978-1-4158-7127-0
Item: 005430351

Dewey Decimal Classification Number: 222.11
Subject Heading: BIBLE. O.T. GENESIS—STUDY \ GOSPEL \ CREATION

Printed in the United States of America.

Leadership and Adult Publishing
LifeWay Church Resources
One LifeWay Plaza
Nashville, Tennessee 37234-0175

We believe the Bible has God for its author; salvation for its end; and truth, without any mixture of error, for its matter and that all Scripture is totally true and trustworthy. The 2000 statement of *The Baptist Faith and Message* is our doctrinal guideline.

Cover design by Matt Lehman

TABLE OF CONTENTS

ICON LEGEND

 Things to listen to

 Things to watch

 Expanding on biblical concepts

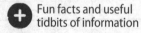 Fun facts and useful tidbits of information

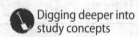 Digging deeper into study concepts

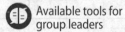 Available tools for group leaders

 On the Web

MEET THE AUTHORS
MATT CARTER

My name is Matt Carter. I serve as pastor for preaching and vision at The Austin Stone Community Church, which has grown from a core team of 15 people to more than 7,000 Sunday attendees since the church began in 2002. My desire to see the church become an advocate for the welfare of the city of Austin has led to the creation of a network that exists to actively pursue the redemption and renewal of the city for the advancement of the gospel. The For the City Network provides a platform for organizational collaboration by offering physical space to local nonprofits and creating a funnel for volunteer engagement. In addition to pastoring at The Austin Stone, I'm a cancer survivor, co-author of *For the City*, and speaker for camps and conferences nationwide. I hold a Master of Divinity from Southwestern Baptist Theological Seminary. I'm married to Jennifer, and we have three children: John Daniel, Annie, and Samuel.

HALIM SUH

Jesus Christ saved me. That's my story. God called me by His grace and won my rebellious heart forever. I am Halim Suh, and I serve as the pastor of equipping at The Austin Stone. I met my wife, Angela, at Texas A&M University. We met, dated, broke up (she with me), dated again (she came to her senses), and got married in 2002. Following college and marriage, I got a Master of Divinity from Southwestern Baptist Theological Seminary. After five years of marriage, we decided it was time to add some children to our family when we got the news that my mom's cancer had returned and would most likely be terminal. We prayed that God would grace us with a child before my mom went to be with Jesus. God answered our prayers, and Malachi was born three months before my mom passed away. Since then God has blessed us with two more children, our daughter Evangeline (Evie) and our son Moses (Mojo). We look forward to adding a couple more kiddos to our family through adoption.

GOD IS MAKING IT GOOD AGAIN

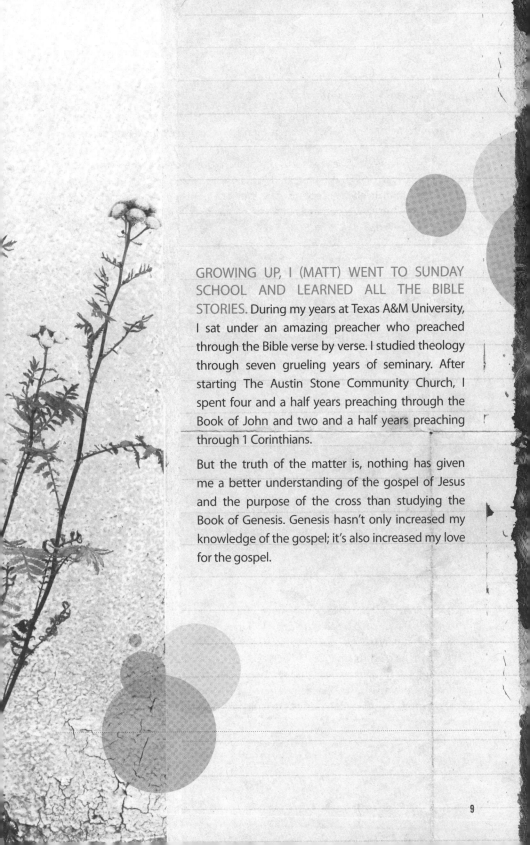

GROWING UP, I (MATT) WENT TO SUNDAY SCHOOL AND LEARNED ALL THE BIBLE STORIES. During my years at Texas A&M University, I sat under an amazing preacher who preached through the Bible verse by verse. I studied theology through seven grueling years of seminary. After starting The Austin Stone Community Church, I spent four and a half years preaching through the Book of John and two and a half years preaching through 1 Corinthians.

But the truth of the matter is, nothing has given me a better understanding of the gospel of Jesus and the purpose of the cross than studying the Book of Genesis. Genesis hasn't only increased my knowledge of the gospel; it's also increased my love for the gospel.

THE BEGINNING . . .

One of the reasons the Book of Genesis advances the gospel in such a powerful way is that it includes the full history of God's story: creation, fall, redemption, and restoration.

The first two chapters of Genesis focus on creation. God looked at the earth that was formless and void, dark and barren, and He chose to create. He spoke, and instantly galaxies came forth in obedience to His voice. With one word from His mouth, the heavens assembled, the oceans were poured out, and mountains emerged from the earth to point back toward heaven.

When God saw everything He had made, He proclaimed, "It is good" (Genesis 1:25). And it was. It was a landscape full of created things and beings erupting with praises for their Creator. Each element of creation was designed to display a different glimpse of His character. In fact, what made creation so good wasn't just that it was beautiful and majestic, but primarily that it pointed to a good, perfect God.

OUR FIRST PARENTS EXPERIENCED EXACTLY WHAT WE WERE CREATED TO BE, AND EVERY ONE OF THEIR NEEDS WAS MET IN GOD.

And yet, even with the billion-fold wonder of stars and the breathtaking majesty of mountains, the best of God's handiwork was revealed when He made man in His own image.

The decision to have men and women not only point to His character but actually bear His image gave humankind the greatest dignity in all creation. When God stepped back after breathing life into His image-bearers, He looked at everything He had made and proclaimed it to be "very good" (v. 31). And it was. In the moments following that proclamation, God and humans enjoyed sweet, intimate communion. Our first parents experienced exactly what we were created to be, and every one of their needs was met in God.

Then came the second phase: The fall.

In Genesis 3-11, the sharp knife of sin severed us from everything that gave us life. In one catastrophic exchange, humanity traded everything God had provided and promised for the lie that they were better off without Him. The serpent convinced Adam and Eve that God was holding out on them—that He couldn't be trusted. The serpent led them to believe that if they wanted true happiness, they would have to do the one thing God had commanded them not to do. The promise from the serpent was that life would be found in this rebellion; the promise from God was that this rebellion would bring death.

BEGINNING IN GENESIS 12 AND CONTINUING THROUGH THE END OF THE BOOK, WE BEGIN TO SEE GOD'S PLAN FOR FIXING WHAT WAS BROKEN. WE SEE HIM BEGIN TO MAKE THE BAD THINGS COME UNTRUE.

Unfortunately, the serpent's lie sounded sweeter to their ears. Everything about abandoning God and going after His throne seemed more appealing. So Adam and Eve rebelled; they took and ate. They traded roles with God Himself and sought in their own power to be their own gods.

The consequences were devastating. Our earliest ancestors were cut off from the paradise of Eden. More importantly, they were cut off from the paradise of knowing God intimately and walking with Him. They were cast out. From that moment on, their hearts were rebelliously bent away from God.

And that's not just Adam and Eve. This is you and me. From the moment we were conceived, we inherited the same stony, dead hearts that beat in the chests of our first parents. Because of their sin *and* because of our own, we're doubly guilty before our Father. We're all sinners by nature and by choice.

. . . AND THE END

Because of the fall, we've been left with a series of terrifying questions: Can we avoid being cut off from God forever? Is there a way to reconcile? Can God look upon us again and declare that we're "very good"?

Thank God, the answer to all of those questions is yes.

Beginning in Genesis 12 and continuing through the end of the book, we get a glimpse of God's plan for fixing what we broke. We see Him making all the bad things come untrue.

Through the stories of Abraham, Jacob, and Joseph, we discover what God intends to accomplish during the remaining phases of our story—redemption and restoration. And it's *very* good.

FOR FURTHER STUDY

Be sure to check out *Creation Unraveled*, the first of our two studies on the gospel according to Genesis. In that book, we walk you through a high-level, big-picture study of Genesis 1-11. Visit *threadsmedia.com/creationunraveled* to find out more, and to continue your study on this vital and valuable topic.

FAITH IS GOD'S DECISIVE ACT

GENESIS 12

SESSION ONE

"By faith Abraham, when he was called, obeyed and went out to a place he was going to receive as an inheritance. He went out, not knowing where he was going. . . . Therefore from one man—in fact, from one as good as dead—came offspring as numerous as the stars of heaven and as innumerable as the grains of sand by the seashore" (Hebrews 11:8,12).

One of the most important things to remember about the Bible is that it's *not* a collection of different stories, each with different moral principles that teach us how to make ourselves right with God. Rather, the Bible is a single, seamless, passionate story about the way God has come down to us.

The second half of Genesis 11 represents a crucial intersection for that story. It's a game-changing moment that confirms God's promise to stop at nothing to redeem His people. And it's a good thing, because the earlier parts of Genesis include some pretty rough stuff.

The problems started in Genesis 3, when sin entered the world and turned all of creation upside down—and not the funny, benign sort of "upside down." Sin ravaged and mauled creation to the point where it was almost indistinguishable from its original state. That same sin launched humanity on a downward spiral that grew with each generation, exponentially magnifying the effects of evil within the hearts of human beings.

God used the flood (Genesis 6-8) and the scattering at the Tower of Babel (Genesis 11) as levies to slow down the viral spread of evil. Those acts of God proved effective at decelerating sin, but they weren't sufficient to eradicate it—nor did God mean for them to be the final solution.

Rather, God had promised that a seed—a person—would come through Eve that would crush the head of Satan and defeat sin once and for all (see Genesis 3:15). This seed would accomplish what the flood, the Tower of Babel, the sacrificial system, and the Law could never do: finally and fully destroy sin within the heart of Man.

To prepare for that seed, God preserved a line of people for Himself—a family of promise through which the Messiah would ultimately be born in Bethlehem. Thus, in the face of murderous Cain and his jealous destruction of Abel, God provided Seth and preserved the line. Atop the tumultuous waters of the flood, God ordained an ark to save Noah and his family, including Shem, who continued the lineage of the promise.

MR. AND MRS. BARREN
In Genesis 11:10, we see a dramatic shift in the narration of the story.

Moses (the author of Genesis) significantly narrows his focus in order to list the many descendants of Shem. With great care and attention to detail, he begins with Shem's first son, Arpachshad, and traces the family line over hundreds of years until he stops at a man named Abram, who would later be re-named Abraham.

Listen to "The One Thing" by Paul Coleman from the *Creation Restored* playlist, available at *threadsmedia.com/creationrestored*.

It's through Abraham that God will continue his chosen family—the line through which He will fulfill His greatest promise to humankind (see Matthew 1).

That being the case, surely we can expect good things from Abraham. We've met a lot of shady characters in Genesis so far—from Cain to Lamech to everybody not named Noah— but at least we can count on Abraham to pray every day, obey God in everything, and live a life of righteousness.

Let's take a look:

> "Terah took his son Abram, his grandson Lot (Haran's son), and his daughter-in-law Sarai, his son Abram's wife, and they set out together from Ur of the Chaldeans to go to the land of Canaan. But when they came to Haran, they settled there" (v. 31).

Uh oh. Ur of the Chaldeans wasn't exactly the flagship city for godly living—not even close. The Chaldeans were a nasty, impetuous people known for their idolatry, and Ur was the capital city of moon worship. Abraham must have been different. Certainly he wasn't into something as silly and destructive as worshiping the moon. Right?

> "Joshua said to all the people, 'This is what the LORD, the God of Israel, says: "Long ago your ancestors, including Terah, the father of Abraham and Nahor, lived beyond the Euphrates River and worshiped other gods"'" (Joshua 24:2).

Oh boy. Abraham participated in idol worship. That takes the wind out of our sails. Abraham is supposed to be the superhero of our faith—the father of faith itself. Yet when we meet him, he is just another guy worshiping something other than God.

Things must have been better for his wife. Maybe Sarah (she was originally called Sarai) was the spiritual one:

> "Abram and Nahor took wives: Abram's wife was named Sarai, and Nahor's wife was named Milcah. She was the daughter of Haran, the father of both Milcah and Iscah. Sarai was unable to conceive; she did not have a child" (Genesis 11:29-30).

What! Sarah couldn't have children? Think about that: Abraham's wife, the woman who was supposed to carry the seed for the next child to be born in God's holy line, was barren. They were both barren, actually, it's just that Abraham's barrenness was spiritual (worshiping what was dead and unproductive) while Sarah's was physical.

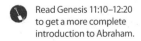 Read Genesis 11:10–12:20 to get a more complete introduction to Abraham.

Reading about Abraham and Sarah's condition, we're forced to wonder why God would choose to work through such a couple instead of picking out a man and woman who better represented the best of what human beings can achieve.

Here's the truth: Because of the presence of sin and its consequences in our lives, barrenness is the perfect metaphor for the human condition. Though we have air in our lungs and a pulse beating throughout our bodies, we can produce no life. We aren't capable of life-giving, or even of true life-living. On our own, the best we can achieve is nothing.

We all have times when we feel the bleakness of our situation. In the midst of this lifelessness and darkness, we want to know if things can get better. Is there hope? Can there be salvation?

We must remember that sin is a great enemy, but God is an even greater Conqueror. Because of God, we do have hope. Because of God, we can experience salvation. But such things don't come from the righteousness of people, or the accomplishment of people, or from being born into the right bloodline.

The amazing news of the gospel is that salvation comes through faith.

That's what was so special about Abraham. He's not one of our spiritual heroes because he lived a perfect life from the beginning. It's because God showed up on the dark landscape of Abraham's life and produced something inside of him—something that changed the course of human history forever.

How do you define faith?

GOD'S WORD PRODUCES FAITH

The apostle Paul has a lot to say about Abraham's faith in Romans 4:18-21:

> **"He believed, hoping against hope, so that he became the father of many nations according to what had been spoken: So will your descendants be. He considered his own body to be already dead (since he was about 100 years old) and also considered the deadness of Sarah's womb, without weakening in the faith. He did not waver in unbelief at God's promise but was strengthened in his faith and gave glory to God, because he was fully convinced that what He had promised He was also able to perform."**

 In 1 Samuel 1:1-20, Hannah's story demonstrates the pain and shame associated with barrenness in the ancient world.

         SESSION ONE CREATION RESTORED

That's a wonderful phrase: "He believed, hoping against hope." Abraham didn't waver in unbelief, but instead grew strong in faith. It's incredible that the same idolator we were just reading about changed to the point where he didn't waver in unbelief at all. Even the strongest of Christians wrestle daily with fear and doubt, yet Abraham moved from trusting idols to trusting God seemingly in the blink of an eye. How?

Maybe Abraham was smarter than the rest of humanity at the time; he just figured things out and decided to turn toward the God he had been rejecting. Or perhaps there was a genetic anomaly in his DNA that predisposed him to have faith—or maybe he was a better guy than all the other people around him.

If you're a follower of Jesus, how did you come to have faith?

Genesis 12 helps us better understand the origin of the faith that sprang up in Abraham's life, even in the midst of his spiritual barrenness:

> "The LORD said to Abram: 'Go out from your land, your relatives, and your father's house to the land that I will show you. I will make you into a great nation, I will bless you, I will make your name great, and you will be a blessing. I will bless those who bless you, I will curse those who treat you with contempt, and all the peoples on earth will be blessed through you.' So Abram went, as the LORD had told him, and Lot went with him. Abram was 75 years old when he left Haran" (vv. 1-4).

This was an important moment. God was kick-starting the next phase in His plan to save the world.

The interaction is strikingly uncomplicated: God spoke, and Abram obeyed. That's all. Abram didn't believe, but God spoke to him and something happened. In the wake of the barren, lifeless void that was the human condition, God spoke—and it changed everything.

Does that sound familiar?

> "In the beginning God created the heavens and the earth. Now the earth was formless and empty, darkness covered the surface of the watery depths, and the Spirit of God was hovering over the surface of the waters. Then God said, 'Let there be light,' and there was light" (Genesis 1:1-3).

 "Now faith is the reality of what is hoped for, the proof of what is not seen " (Hebrews 11:1).

Compare the texts from Genesis 12 and Genesis 1. What are the similarities? What are the differences?

Notice what the Word of God shows us: Both instances started with nothing, and in both instances God spoke and created something that wasn't there before. In Genesis 1 God's powerful voice brought light into the dark void of our world. In Genesis 12, our world was void of faith in the one, true God, but then God spoke. And He spoke in such a way that His Word, His promises, created faith inside of Abraham.

Abraham wasn't perfect. He didn't earn the right to have faith from God by being intelligent, charming, or even godly. Abraham had faith because God decided to speak His Word into his life.

That's our story, too.

If you have faith to believe God and put your trust in Him, it's because He called you to do so. God Himself opened His mouth and produced the very faith you cling to. That may not be something you've spent a lot of time contemplating before now, but it's real. It's something Paul addressed in his second letter to the Corinthians:

> "For God who said, 'Let light shine out of darkness,' has shone in our hearts to give the light of the knowledge of God's glory in the face of Jesus Christ" (2 Corinthians 4:6).

So who's the Hero here? Who's the One who can take credit for creating light in the midst of darkness? Or faith in the midst of the darkest hearts?

God.

God is responsible for creating faith in His people, and He wants us to know it. There's no other way out of our peril. There's no other person strong enough and loving enough to help. We're not the heroes of our stories, no matter how much we want to be (or how much we act like it).

How do you respond to the idea that God is responsible for our faith, rather than our actions or decisions?

Watch the *Creation Restored* video
"Faith Is God's Decisive Act," available
at *threadsmedia.com/creationrestored*.

Walter Brueggemann says it well in his commentary on the Book of Genesis:

> "This family (and with it the whole family of Genesis 1–11) has played out its future and has nowhere else to go. Barrenness is the way of human history. It is an effective metaphor for hopelessness. There is no foreseeable future. There is no human power to invent a future.

> "But barrenness is not only the condition of hopeless humanity. The marvel of biblical faith is that barrenness is the arena of God's life-giving action. . . .

> "Inexplicably, this God speaks His powerful word directly into a situation of barrenness. That is the ground of the good news. This God does not depend on any potentiality in the one addressed. . . . The speech of God presumes nothing from the one addressed but carries in itself all that is necessary to begin a new people in history. The power of this summoning word is without analogy. It is a word about the future spoken to this family without any hope of a future. . . . The remainder of the text is simply the announcement that the speech of God overcomes and overpowers the barrenness of human reality."[1]

GOD'S WORD DEFINES FAITH

If we can get on board with the fact that God's Word was the genesis (pun intended) of faith for Abraham, then we've answered the question of where faith originated. And that answer is key because it means God, and God alone, gets the credit for our salvation.

But this leads us to more questions that may be equally important: What is faith? What does it mean to have faith? How do we know the faith we're holding onto is the same faith God created in Abraham—not something counterfeit or counterproductive?

Thankfully, God's Word goes beyond *producing* faith in us; it also *defines* faith for us. And we can learn more by looking again at our friend Abraham. He is an example of the life that is both demanded by and produced from this kind of genuine, God-spoken faith. We know what faith ought to look like in our lives by watching what God called Abraham to do after giving him the gift of faith.

Faith Is Finding Our Security in God Alone
Let's take a deeper look into those first verses in chapter 12:

> "The LORD said to Abram: 'Go out from your land, your relatives, and your father's house to the land that I will show you'" (v. 1).

First, God called Abraham to leave the people he loved and the place where he felt secure.

Clearly, such a call didn't waste any time beating around the bush. All of the things that could have defined Abraham other than his relationship with God were placed on the chopping block right out of the gate.

Tim Keller offers a good summary of Abraham's situation:

> "Leave . . . your country. He was to let go of his economic and material security. He was leaving a much more settled, 'civilized' environment for a 'backwoods' uncivilized one. He was putting at risk all the normal social advancement to be hoped for. He was leaving all physical and social safety. Leave . . . your people. He was to let go of his cultural security. He left a familiar culture and customs for a foreign society. He was going to a place where he would always be an outsider, never an insider, never comfortable. Leave . . . your father's household. Finally, he was to let go of his personal, emotional security. In traditional cultures one's identity was tied up on your family. He was no longer allowed to rest in the sorts of relationships that we ordinarily get our self-worth and sense of significance from."[2]

Abraham's call had an interesting dynamic. You've probably heard many testimonies of God calling people away from lives of drunkenness and immorality, lewdness and debauchery—bad things, in other words. What's striking about Abraham's call is that he was ordered to leave the good things in his life. He was called to leave anything he trusted in more than God for his security.

That's important. Having faith doesn't mean we lie and curse a little less than we did before. It doesn't mean we stop gossiping. It isn't a commitment to stop lying and lusting once and for all. Faith isn't an attempt to give us the look of morality. That's not faith at all. That isn't Christianity, either.

Having faith in God means letting go of everything that our hands are grasping so tightly in our effort to find identity and security—yes, even seemingly good things—and looking toward God to keep us, instead.

It means that from now on our families, jobs, bank accounts, and so forth don't get to define us—God does. We must be willing to recognize when these good things have stopped being blessings and have shifted into masters that we obey more than God. Otherwise, we'll spend our lives deluding ourselves into believing we trusted God only to realize that we were serving ourselves and our desires more than Him.

 "Any faith that must be supported by the evidence of the senses is not real faith." —A. W. Tozer, *The Knowledge of the Holy*[5]

Where do you currently find physical and economic security?

Where do you find social and cultural security?

Where is the first place you turn for emotional support?

Our hearts are bent toward trusting things other than God, and it's because of the fall. We know there are a million things the world offers for happiness in place of God. We know to be on the lookout for things like lust and impurity. But that isn't all we have to worry about. Our hearts are capable of turning blessings into idols, too. And God is calling us to take an inventory of our hearts and determine if what's inside defines us more than He does.

Faith that is from God both requires us and helps us to find our highest security and identity in Him alone.

Faith Is Committing to Bless the World
True faith calls us to separate ourselves from the things of the world that may tempt us with security. But how are we supposed to do that practically? To what extent do we "leave"?

Most of us aren't called to leave our families and jobs, and surely we're not going to leave our children. Is God commanding us to completely remove ourselves from the world, to have no affiliation or association with anyone else? Are we called to be repulsed by the world and hate it from a distance?

That doesn't sound like our God.

Thankfully, the next statement God made to Abraham clarifies that His heart for the world is quite the opposite.

> "I will make you into a great nation, I will bless you, I will make your name great, and you will be a blessing. I will bless those who bless you, I will curse those who treat you with contempt, and all the peoples on earth will be blessed through you" (Genesis 12:2-3).

The second command God gave Abraham was to be a blessing to the nations. That's a good thing, certainly, but it can be a bit confusing in light of the first command. How could Abraham both separate himself from the things of the world and participate in blessing the world? How can we?

It turns out that God's commands weren't mutually exclusive. Obeying the first actually contributes to accomplishing the second, and that's exactly what God proposed to Abraham: He needed to separate from the nations in order to bless the nations.

God calls us to do the same thing today. We are commanded to be both salt and light (Matthew 5:13-16); we are to be in the world but not of the world. We must be different than the world in order to bless the world.

Here's how Ligon Duncan expresses this concept:

> "As Christians we must distinctively see ourselves as different from the world. We must think differently from the world. We must have a different worldview and outlook from the world. We must have a different set of priorities. We must have a different set of goals. Our agenda is different from the agenda of the world. But we do that not so we can stand over against the world and feel superior to the world. Or despise the world in the sense of not having any concern for the interests of men and women who are not part of the faith. We are distinctive in order that we can be a blessing. In other words, we must say no to the world in order that we can say yes to the world."[3]

That's an interesting idea: We must say *no* to the world so that we can say *yes* to the world. There's a tension there, and we're supposed to live inside of it. We must leave and separate ourselves from the things of the world, and we must seek to bless the world.

Still, that can be a challenging line to walk.

Some of us are great at keeping the command to "leave." In an effort to ensure that we're not mastered by anything or anyone other than God, we isolate ourselves from everything that doesn't overtly communicate His value system. We shield ourselves and our families from anything that isn't found in a Christian bookstore.

That puts us in danger of separating ourselves from the world so much that we lose our ability to look upon it with compassion. We can be so swept away by our efforts to separate that we forget that, apart from God's undeserved grace in our lives, we would be in the same place.

Others of us do a really great job obeying the second commandment to bless the world. In fact, we can have such a heart to see the world be reconciled to Christ that we become just like the world. In the name of tolerance and relatability we start bending our values to those of the world—instead of the other way around.

The danger here is that we can lose our distinctive saltiness. In an effort to move people out of the line of the world and into the line of godliness, we instead just make one line. We pursue all the things that the world pursues, we laugh at the same jokes, and we find pleasure in the same entertainment. As a result, the world doesn't see the need to change because there's no picture of change in front of them.

On which side of the pendulum do you tend to swing? How can you tell?

The challenge for the Christian life is doing both of these things well, like Jesus. He was able to be around some of the most lawless and offensive people in society—people who did not share His value system at all—and yet they wanted to be around Him because of the way He loved them.

We must be able to see the idols the world offers and choose instead to worship God unashamedly. At the same time, we must acknowledge that many people are serving idols because they don't know about the God we serve. They don't know there is a God who desires to save them from the throes of sin and death; they don't know there is a God who crossed heaven and earth to deliver them from the peril of condemnation they live in every day, and the infinitely worse peril of eternal judgment that awaits them if they die in their sins without putting their faith in Him.

Faith is making a commitment, by God's grace, to obey both commands the way Jesus did. It's making a commitment to be separate from the world so that we can bless the world.

Faith Is Trusting God
Let's look back at Genesis 12:1 for another element of genuine faith:

> **"The Lord said to Abram: 'Go out from your land, your relatives, and your father's house to the land that I will show you.'"**

Where does God command Abraham to go? Africa? Somewhere in the 10/40 window? No. God commanded him to go to the land that He would show him. He left everything open-ended.

 According to the *Holman Illustrated Bible Dictionary*, Ur of the Chaldeans (11:28) is identified as Tell el-Muqayyar, 220 miles southeast of Baghdad, Iraq.

It's fair to wonder why God would work that way. He was so specific about the things that should be left behind, so why wouldn't He demonstrate the same level of detail when telling Abraham where to go? It seems like the margin of error is much higher with God being so vague. There were a lot of ways Abraham could mess this up.

But maybe God was less concerned with the destination and Abraham's ability to get there than He was concerned about Abraham trusting Him. The destination of faith wasn't a particular point on the map, but instead a place of trust in Abraham's heart.

That seems to be a key characteristic of faith from this text according to the writer of Hebrews:

> **"By faith Abraham, when he was called, obeyed and went out to a place he was going to receive as an inheritance. He went out, not knowing where he was going" (Hebrews 11:8).**

This has to be one of the hardest aspects of faith for us to handle. It's so counter-intuitive to the way our hearts want to operate since the fall. In fact, that first sin was actually a rebellion against this very quality of faith.

God commanded Adam and Eve to trust Him as the One to determine what was good and bad. And they played along until the snake slithered in and tempted them to sit in God's chair—the place where they would get to make the call for themselves, even if they called it wrong every time. God left the consequences open-ended, too. He didn't tell Adam and Eve all of the horror and pain that would happen if they ate of the fruit. He didn't tell them their disobedience would be the cause of so much misery and torment throughout humankind.

God could have shared that information. He could have made things very clear for Adam and Eve, and who knows—maybe things would have turned out differently. But it would not have been because Adam and Eve trusted God; it would have been because they agreed in their own wisdom that the consequences would be bad.

That wasn't the destination God wanted with Adam and Eve, and it's not the destination He sought for Abraham, either. Both examples required trust in God above anything and anyone else—they required full obedience without fully knowing where God would lead. That's the essence of faith.

When have you been forced to trust in God without knowing where that trust would lead?

Yet some of us get so frustrated with the whole process. *Just tell me what to do and I'll do it, God! Do You want me to move my family to that poor neighborhood so we can serve? Fine. Do You want me to change jobs? OK. Should I sell everything? No problem. Just tell me exactly what You want me to do so I can make it happen. Tell me how to please You and I will. Let's just cut to the chase!*

What kinds of decisions or problems make you feel this way?

God doesn't operate that way. He isn't a cold, overbearing dictator who wants us to robotically accomplish His will on earth for the sake of getting His way. And when we demand for God to tell us exactly what He wants so that we can get out there and do it, we reveal that deep down we see Him as more of a boss than as a Father who loves us.

More, if we only obeyed God when He gave us the entire picture, we wouldn't be operating in faith at all. That's what the writer of Hebrews says:

> "Now faith is the reality of what is hoped for, the proof of what is not seen" (11:1).

Of course, that's exactly what makes authentic faith so challenging. Faith is the work of transforming hopes into assurances—of converting the invisible and unseen into deep and meaningful convictions.

The unknown can make faith so frustrating, but it's also what makes faith so real. And the good news is that "the unknown" is only unknown to us. God knows exactly where He's leading us, and He will lead us there perfectly. He will not only get us to the right place geographically, but the right place in our hearts of trusting Him fully and absolutely.

THE GREAT GAP

Here's a scary thought: Abraham went out, but he never arrived. He never got to see with his own eyes the fulfillment of God's promises. God promised Abraham land, but he never owned any land except his own grave. God promised him a nation, but he didn't even get to see a single grandchild, let alone a nation. God promised him greatness, but he lived in tents all his life.

Abraham lived in the great gap between promise and reality.

And that's where we live, too.

Leading a group? It's the way to go. Find extra questions and teaching tools in the leader kit, available at *threadsmedia.com/creationrestored*.

Yes, God's most critical promise was fulfilled through the death and resurrection of Jesus. But many more promises are still floating around, and the chances are good we'll never see every one fulfilled within our lifetime. Like John Piper says:

> "Faith tastes the blessing of God's goodness now in this age, but not most of it. There is so much yet to come. . . . It will all be, as Paul says, 'through a glass, darkly.' It will all be partial. Every joy will have its limits. Every fruit its bruise. Every relationship its disappointment. Every service its critic. And every birth and wedding its nearby funeral.

> "Hebrews 13:14 takes up the very thought of Abraham's faith: 'Here we have no lasting city.' Everything breaks. Everything ages, spoils, rusts. Only God remains unchanged and glorious."[4]

Getting back to Abraham, we see that 10 years after God called him, the gap between the promise and their fulfillment was starting to wear on him.

> **"After these events, the word of the LORD came to Abram in a vision: 'Do not be afraid, Abram. I am your shield; your reward will be very great.' But Abram said, 'LORD God, what can You give me, since I am childless and the heir of my house is Eliezer of Damascus?' Abram continued, 'Look, You have given me no offspring, so a slave born in my house will be my heir'"** (Genesis 15:1-3).

I can't think of a single person who would have a hard time relating to Abraham here. We've all felt dissatisfied with some of God's promises. He promised to never leave us nor forsake us, for example, but there are definitely times we feel like we've been on our own for a while. He promised to conform us to the image of His Son, but we can't seem to get free from the power of sin. He promised to hear us when we cry out to Him, but there are times when the sky feels like brass, bouncing back our prayers.

What are we supposed to do with these feelings of weariness and fatigue as we wait for God's promises to be fulfilled?

One thing we can do is glean some lessons from Abraham's situation. For instance, notice how God responded to Abraham's frustrated groaning. Did God berate him? Did He withdraw the promise because of Abraham's impatience and frustration?

No, God made a covenant with him.

 "For now we see through a glass, darkly; but then face to face: now I know in part; but then shall I know even as also I am known" (1 Corinthians 13:12, KJV).

In that day, a covenant was traditionally made by two people passing through a bunch of cut-up pieces of animals that were scattered on the ground. The agreement was solidified with the understanding that if one party broke the covenant, then what happened to the animals would happen to them, as well. Both parties were on the hook, and both were subject to the penalty if they broke their promise.

When God makes His covenant with Abraham, however, we see something unique:

> "When the sun had set and it was dark, a smoking fire pot and a flaming torch appeared and passed between the divided animals. On that day the LORD made a covenant with Abram, saying, 'I give this land to your offspring, from the brook of Egypt to the Euphrates River: the land of the Kenites, Kenizzites, Kadmonites, Hittites, Perizzites, Rephaim, Amorites, Canaanites, Girgashites, and Jebusites'" (Genesis 15:17-21).

Who passed between the animal pieces? God alone.

Abraham wondered, *God, how can I know with 100 percent certainty that You're going to fulfill these things You've promised?* And God answered by assuming the full risk of the covenant. He came down from heaven and walked alone through the slaughtered animals as a sign of His faithfulness to Abraham. In other words, if God didn't fulfill His promises, then let His holy, perfect body be chopped into pieces. God was letting Abraham know that *nothing* would stand in the way of His faithfulness.

What about us, though? It was great for Abraham that God came down and gave him such a reminder—but what about those of us in the gap right now? We're tired. We feel like we're hanging on by a very thin thread. We know in our minds that God will keep His promises, but every day that passes in the gap seems to loosen our grip on that trust.

Can't God give us something like the sign He gave to Abraham? We don't see any flaming pots or cut-up animals around here. So how can we know, like Abraham knew, that God will keep His promises?

Here's the answer:

> "And He took bread, gave thanks, broke it, gave it to them, and said, 'This is My body, which is given for you. Do this in remembrance of Me.' In the same way He also took the cup after supper and said, 'This cup is the new covenant established by My blood; it is shed for you'" (Luke 22:19-20).

God answered our question 2,000 years ago not with the blood of bulls and goats, but with the broken body and spilled blood of His only Son.

Long ago God made a promise to Abraham—a promise that carried a price all the way to death. Jesus came to pay that price not only that we might be redeemed from our sins, but that we would know, without a doubt in our minds, that no power in all the universe can keep us from receiving the promised blessings of God.

When you feel yourself in the gap of unfulfilled promises—when you start getting weary—look to the cross. Let your heart be overwhelmed by what God has done to fulfill His promise to Abraham and to us. Jesus went to the cross so that you never have to wonder if He loves you.

What steps can you take to follow this advice?

MOVING FORWARD

True faith can only come from God, and there are certain qualities that distinguish it as genuine:

- Finding your security in God alone
- Committing to bless the nations
- Trusting God in spite of open-ended instructions

Maybe you've read all this and you feel overwhelmed. You're thinking: *That's just too hard!*

If so, you're actually in pretty good shape. Because genuine faith is supposed to be too hard for us. Remember that God made many promises to Abraham—He promised land, a nation, a great name. But all of those promises were hinged on one, specific pledge: that Abraham would have a son.

Abraham's only hope was in the son God had promised. And that's our only hope, as well.

> **"For all the promises of God find their Yes in him. That is why it is through him that we utter our Amen to God for his glory" (2 Corinthians 1:20, ESV).**

If you're feeling like you'll never be able to believe and trust God like you're supposed to, you're forgetting something very important: Someone has already believed and trusted perfectly for you.

Jesus, the true Son of promise, answered the call of God. He went out from heaven; He left the ultimate Father's house and came to be born into the poverty of fallen creation. He left His perfect heavenly country for the busted country of humanity. Sin was something that He never knew, and yet He became a sin offering so that we might become the righteousness of God in Him (see Romans 8:3, below).

Jesus became fatherless as He cried out, "My God! My God! Why have You forsaken Me!" (Mark 15:34). He lost His Father so that we could gain the Father. He lost His country so that we might gain a new citizenship in heaven. He became a curse so that we could become a royal priesthood. He lost everything that we might gain God.

That's why we can have hope.

That's what faith is all about.

APPLY TO LIFE

Make it a point to concentrate on the concept of faith this week. To start, use the space on pages 30-31 to write down, in your own words, a definition for faith. Also write down the origin of your faith in God (or lack thereof)—when and where did it start?

Throughout the week, make a mental note every time you are in a situation that requires faith of any kind—faith in God, faith in a coworker, faith in a mechanic, and so on. (If you can, carry a notebook with you and make actual notes rather than keeping everything in your head.) At the end of the week, review your notes and answer these questions:

1. What was surprising about your experiences?
2. What was confusing or troubling?
3. What conclusions can you make about the strength and trajectory of your ability to have faith in general?
4. What conclusions can you make about the strength and trajectory of your faith in God?

Spark a conversation with a friend or spouse this week by asking, "Do you think I'm a person of faith? Why or why not?"

 "What the law could not do since it was limited by the flesh, God did. He condemned sin in the flesh by sending His own Son in flesh like ours under sin's domain, and as a sin offering" (Romans 8:3).

FAITH IS OUR DEPENDENT ACT

GENESIS 18–19

SESSION TWO

"All of us have become like **something unclean**, and all our righteous acts are like a polluted garment; all of us wither like a leaf, and our iniquities carry us away like the wind. No one calls on Your name, striving to take hold of You. For You have hidden Your face from us and made us melt because of our iniquity" (Isaiah 64:6-7).

Some people perceive the Bible to be a male-centered collection of books—and there's some truth to that given the patriarchal cultures in which those books were written. It's also true that a high percentage of biblical scholarship has been conducted by men throughout the history of the church, which has at times influenced things toward a masculine perspective.

But when we actually dig into the pages of Scripture, we find them bursting with the actions and sentiments of women. What's more, we find women who are vitally important to God's redemptive purposes in our world.

That's the case with Sarah in Genesis 18, and we'll begin this session by looking at her reaction to the promise of a child.

LAUGHING AT THE PROMISES OF GOD
Things got started with a surprising visit:

> "Then the LORD appeared to Abraham at the oaks of Mamre while he was sitting in the entrance of his tent during the heat of the day. He looked up, and he saw three men standing near him. When he saw them, he ran from the entrance of the tent to meet them and bowed to the ground. Then he said, 'My lord, if I have found favor in your sight, please do not go on past your servant. Let a little water be brought, that you may wash your feet and rest yourselves under the tree. I will bring a bit of bread so that you may strengthen yourselves. This is why you have passed your servant's way. Later, you can continue on'" (Genesis 18:1-5).

Obviously this was a special occasion, although Sarah was confined to the tent:

> "So Abraham hurried into the tent and said to Sarah, 'Quick! Knead three measures of fine flour and make bread.' Meanwhile, Abraham ran to the herd and got a tender, choice calf. He gave it to a young man, who hurried to prepare it. Then Abraham took curds and milk, and the calf that he had prepared, and set them before the men. He served them as they ate under the tree" (vv. 6-8).

Imagine performing some mundane chore and then, out of nowhere, your husband runs in like a madman and tells you to make a bunch of cakes. Then he sprints out again, and you come to find out he's throwing steaks on the grill because God has dropped by for a visit.

....

Listen to "Legacy" by Nichole Nordeman
from the *Creation Restored* playlist, available
at *threadsmedia.com/creationrestored*.

How would you have responded if you were in Sarah's shoes?

Have you ever felt excluded from spiritual occasions or opportunities? What emotions did you experience?

Watch what happened next. While Abraham and God were under the shade tree, visiting, eating, and having a good time, God intentionally turned the conversation toward Sarah:

> "'Where is your wife Sarah?' they asked him. 'There, in the tent,' he answered. The LORD said, 'I will certainly come back to you in about a year's time, and your wife Sarah will have a son!'

> "Now Sarah was listening at the entrance of the tent behind him. Abraham and Sarah were old and getting on in years. Sarah had passed the age of childbearing. So she laughed to herself: 'After I have become shriveled up and my lord is old, will I have delight?'" (vv. 9-12).

Up to this point in the text, the promise of a son had been directed toward Abraham, and we've seen Abraham's response. But now God switches the emphasis and highlights the reality that Sarah will have the son. This is the same promise we saw in Genesis 12—with the added info that it will be fulfilled "in about a year's time"—yet we get to see what the woman who will actually bear the child thinks of the entire situation.

The text makes it pretty clear Sarah wasn't buying it.

To be fair, Sarah had a legitimate reason for skepticism. We are told that "Sarah had passed the age of childbearing," which means she had gone through menopause. Biologically speaking, she was not able to have children.

Describe a situation in which your faith clashed with what seemed like common sense. What was the result?

In light of all this, how did Sarah respond to this promise from God? She laughed out loud.

....

 Read Genesis 13–17 to see how Abraham rescued Lot, Hagar gave birth to Ishmael, and God instituted the covenant of circumcision.

Joy Deferred

We know through the narrative of Genesis that Sarah desperately wanted to have a son. She had tried everything. Nothing had panned out the way she hoped, and now she was barren and post-menopausal.

Imagine trying everything in your earthly power to control or change a situation, and then finally giving up because you're exhausted from the wasted effort and you realize it's too late for your dream to come true. If someone walked up one day and told you the dream would come true, would you laugh, too?

Maybe that's where you are right now. Maybe there are things you've wanted for a long time, things you've been searching the world to find—happiness, joy, significance, approval, acceptance, love, and more. And you've come up short. Maybe you're tired, too. You know God has promised in His Word to fulfill those longings in the depths of your heart, but the thought of finally having something you've worked toward for so long seems almost comical.

What are you hoping for right now that fits these descriptions?

If you can relate, then learn from Sarah.

In that moment, Sarah's circumstances were more real to her than anything else. All she could see was everything that had stood in her way in the past—every obstacle, every weakness, every lost day that confirmed her inability to have what she truly wanted. Even when God came and sat on her front porch, she couldn't see Him past her miserable circumstances. In her mind they were too big to overcome even by the Most High Himself.

Watch what happened next:

> **"But the LORD asked Abraham, 'Why did Sarah laugh, saying, "Can I really have a baby when I'm old?" Is anything impossible for the LORD? At the appointed time I will come back to you, and in about a year she will have a son'" (Genesis 18:13-14).**

Busted. In His omniscience, God knew Sarah laughed, but He didn't seem offended by Sarah's doubts. He didn't react by taking away the promise or by postponing when she would receive it. No, He reminded her of what was true—that *nothing* is too hard for Him. Then He restated the promise without changing a thing.

Head vs. Heart

"Is anything impossible for the LORD?" We all need to consider that question.

Of course, we know the answer in our heads; we know what we're supposed to say. But have we forgotten the truth in our hearts? Do our lives testify that we truly believe nothing is too hard for God? Or has that promise been lost because it's been so misused over the years?

Understand something: Nothing is too hard for God, but the Bible is not prescribing this promise as a magic trick to make God do whatever we want Him to do. We can't just apply this idea across whatever realm of life we want to and manipulate God like a genie. He doesn't promise we'll win football games or pass tests we didn't study for. This verse is not for all the things we want God to do for us.

No, this verse is for us to remember that *what He has promised*, He will accomplish.

Also notice that the content of the promise didn't change with Sarah's unbelieving laugh. Not even our unbelief can keep God from accomplishing what He promises.

God's question to Sarah is the same question for you today. He wants you to know that if He has promised something to you, then there is nothing that will stand in the way of Him remaining faithful to that promise. No matter how difficult the situation, no matter how daunting the circumstances—nothing is too hard for Him. He wants us to believe Him more than we believe our circumstances.

What problems have you encountered recently that seem too difficult to handle?

So, what happened with Sarah? Let's pick up the story a year later:

> "The LORD came to Sarah as He had said, and the LORD did for Sarah what He had promised. Sarah became pregnant and bore a son to Abraham in his old age, at the appointed time God had told him. Abraham named his son who was born to him—the one Sarah bore to him—Isaac. When his son Isaac was eight days old, Abraham circumcised him, as God had commanded him. Abraham was 100 years old when his son Isaac was born to him. Sarah said, 'God has made me laugh, and everyone who hears will laugh with me.' She also said, 'Who would have told Abraham that Sarah would nurse children? Yet I have borne a son for him in his old age'" (Genesis 21:1-7).

 Genesis 5 mentions four fathers who were older than Abraham when they had children: Seth, Jared, Methuselah, and Lamech.

Sarah laughed again, but this time she wasn't laughing out of cynicism or skepticism; she wasn't mocking God. This time she was rocking her baby in her arms, the baby she never would have had without God keeping His promise. She was staring at the promise and power of God with her own eyes, seeing His faithfulness more tangibly than she ever had before—more than her circumstances, for sure.

And in that moment, she laughed. Overwhelmed by God's faithfulness and power, she laughed out of awe. She laughed in wonder. The promise came true; her God had come through. God had birthed the same faith in Sarah through His spoken promise that He had birthed in Abraham.

Every time she saw her boy running around the yard or called his name, she must have remembered: Nothing is impossible for my God.

Here's something else that's funny: The name Isaac means "laughter."

What regularly reminds you of God's faithfulness?

GRACE FOR SODOM AND GOMORRAH

Since we're talking about God keeping His promises, let's shift our attention to the people of Sodom and Gomorrah. They also received a promise from God, although theirs was not so happy. The promise hanging over those people and their city was that God is holy and just; He will always punish sin and punish it severely.

Immediately after the conversation between God and Abraham under the shade tree about Sarah and her future child, God brought up the topic of Sodom and Gomorrah:

> "Then the LORD said, 'The outcry against Sodom and Gomorrah is immense, and their sin is extremely serious. I will go down to see if what they have done justifies the cry that has come up to Me. If not, I will find out.' The men turned from there and went toward Sodom while Abraham remained standing before the LORD" (Genesis 18:20-22).

When Abraham heard this, I'm sure his heart skipped a few beats. He had family there. His nephew Lot, along with all of the members of Lot's household, lived in Sodom. As a result, Abraham did something incredibly bold. He stood before God and pled for a city; he asked God to pardon the accused and spare them from destruction.

Watch the *Creation Restored* video
"Faith Is Our Dependent Act," available
at *threadsmedia.com/creationrestored*.

> "Abraham stepped forward and said, 'Will You really sweep away the righteous with the wicked? What if there are 50 righteous people in the city? Will You really sweep it away instead of sparing the place for the sake of the 50 righteous people who are in it? You could not possibly do such a thing: to kill the righteous with the wicked, treating the righteous and the wicked alike. You could not possibly do that! Won't the Judge of all the earth do what is just?'" (Genesis 18:23-25).

If we were watching this scene as a movie, this would be the time for a dramatic gasp—although our culture often prevents us from seeing it that way. In fact, for those of us who are Americans, this may not seem like a crazy request at all. It probably makes a lot of sense. That perspective prevents us from recognizing the magnitude of what happened.

In that moment, Abraham asked God to do something that was totally new. Abraham asked God *not* to punish sin.

Up to that point in human history, God had dealt pretty thoroughly with sin. He had been operating on a principle called guilt transference, which is a lot like the concept of "guilt by association." It means that when the *one* is guilty, the consequences are transferred to the *many*. This can be tough for us to grasp because we have a very individualistic mind-set, but that's the way God designed things to work.

Paul discussed this a bit in the New Testament:

> "Therefore, just as sin entered the world through one man, and death through sin, in this way death spread to all men, because all sinned" (Romans 5:12).

Is the boldness of Abraham's request starting to set in?

Abraham might as well have said: "God, will You not punish the sinners based on the fact that there are some righteous people in the city? Instead of bringing destruction because of the sin of many, will You spare the many on account of the righteousness of the few? I know that you typically enact guilt transference, God, but would You be willing to use righteousness transference instead?"

The only thing more remarkable than Abraham's request is the fact that God said yes.

> "The LORD said, 'If I find 50 righteous people in the city of Sodom, I will spare the whole place for their sake'" (Genesis 18:26).

 In Exodus 32:11-14, Moses offered a similar prayer on behalf of the Israelites after they worshiped the golden calf.

That statement is a *huge* glimpse into the gospel! God made a way for sinners to be saved, but it requires that a righteous person be found in the midst of those the sinners.

Abraham realized a problem, though, and it hit him like a ton of bricks: What if 50 righteous people weren't found within those two cities? As a result, he launched into a long-winded series of hypothetical questions with God to determine just how many righteous people would have to be found in order to save the cities.

> "Then Abraham answered, 'Since I have ventured to speak to the Lord— even though I am dust and ashes—suppose the 50 righteous lack five. Will you destroy the whole city for lack of five?' He replied, 'I will not destroy it if I find 45 there.' Then he spoke to Him again, 'Suppose 40 are found there?' He answered, 'I will not do it on account of 40.' Then he said, 'Let the Lord not be angry, and I will speak further. Suppose 30 are found there?' He answered, 'I will not do it if I find 30 there.' Then he said, 'Since I have ventured to speak to the Lord, suppose 20 are found there?' He replied, 'I will not destroy it on account of 20.' Then he said, 'Let the Lord not be angry, and I will speak one more time. Suppose 10 are found there?' He answered, 'I will not destroy it on account of 10'" (Genesis 18:27-32).

Obviously this was a case of high-stakes haggling, but notice what happened after Abraham hit the number 10: He stopped pleading with the Lord on behalf of the city. Why didn't he keep going? You get the sense from the way things were playing out that if Abraham had continued to just one righteous person, God would have agreed to spare Sodom and Gomorrah.

Whether or not he realized it, Abraham stumbled onto one of the central truths of Scripture: There weren't going to be any righteous people in Sodom and Gomorrah because there aren't any righteous people anywhere. Not even one.

> "As it is written: There is no one righteous, not even one. There is no one who understands; there is no one who seeks God. All have turned away; all alike have become useless. There is no one who does what is good, not even one" (Romans 3:10-12).

The only hope for Sodom and Gomorrah to be spared was finding someone who was righteous, who had not turned away and rejected God. God was ready to pour out His grace on those two cities, if only someone could transfer his or her righteousness to the ungodly. But who could stand in the gap and claim the perfection that was necessary to satisfy God?

There were no such people within Sodom and Gomorrah. Not 50, not 30, not 10, not 5, not even 1. And from the text we know that God did what He said He would do—He punished their sin by destroying both cities (see Genesis 19).

Think back to when you first heard the story of Sodom and Gomorrah. How did you react at the time?

How do you react now when you read about the destruction of cities and their inhabitants?

God keeps His promises. That happened to be bad news for the sinners in Sodom and Gomorrah, and sometimes it's bad news for sinners like us. Because God keeps His promises, we know the fate of Sodom and Gomorrah would have been our fate if a righteous person had never been found.

The good news is that our God made another promise—one that went all the way back to that terrible day when sin first entered the world:

> **"I will put hostility between you and the woman, and between your seed and her seed. He will strike your head, and you will strike his heel"** (Genesis 3:15).

God promised that one day He would send a Messiah, the ultimate Seed, who was perfectly righteous and holy in the midst of a world full of nothing but sinners.

That's Jesus.

The lesson from Sodom and Gomorrah isn't that there were really bad sinners and God was ready to destroy those really bad sinners. The lesson is that you and I are no different from Sodom and Gomorrah. We deserve to be destroyed, but God desires to save us—not because of our righteousness but because of the righteousness of another.

We must look to Jesus for our righteousness. He is the only righteous Person who can raise His hand and give us what He has earned through a perfect life of obedience. Our only hope is to point to Jesus and trust Him for that righteousness.

 Listen to "Show Up" by Jill Phillips from the *Creation Restored* playlist, available at *threadsmedia.com/creationrestored.*

THE MAN IN THE MIDDLE

So far in this study we've looked at two ends of a spectrum—two contrasting examples of faith and obedience.

In Abraham we saw a man who had great faith birthed into him. As a result, he left everything and followed God, even when it cost him everything he held dear. He's a clear example of what it looks like to receive and rely upon faith to obey God's commands.

In Sodom and Gomorrah we saw complete disobedience and utter rejection of God. The people of those cities went their own way and reveled in immorality, pride, and greed. They're a clear example of what it looks like to have faith in ourselves and the things of the world.

But there's another character wedged between those two examples, and he can be easy to miss. That would be Lot, Abraham's nephew.

Lot is an example of a person who found himself somewhere between Abraham and the people of Sodom and Gomorrah. He was a believer who tried to pursue both God and the things of the world, which makes it easy for most Christians to relate to him.

We get a first glimpse of Lot's attitude in Genesis 13. At that point in the story, Abraham and Lot were living and journeying together in obedience to God. They had both left their home and family, and they were heading toward the land God had promised. That's when Lot saw an opportunity:

> "Lot looked out and saw that the entire Jordan Valley as far as Zoar was well watered everywhere like the LORD's garden and the land of Egypt. This was before the LORD destroyed Sodom and Gomorrah. So Lot chose the entire Jordan Valley for himself. Then Lot journeyed eastward, and they separated from each other. Abram lived in the land of Canaan, but Lot lived in the cities of the valley and set up his tent near Sodom" (Genesis 13:10-12).

Instead of walking by faith, like Abraham, Lot walked by sight. The text is clear about this: it emphasizes that he "looked out and saw." The plains of the Jordan River near Sodom were rich and fertile. The land was great for cattle and pastures. From a logical, rational perspective, this was a great move for Lot. And so, with no regard for God's promise, without consulting the Lord, Lot split away from Abraham and moved toward Sodom.

What factors do you consider when making major life decisions?

 The 2005 book *Soul Searching*, by Christian Smith, revealed that most young people view religion in terms of "Moralistic Therapeutic Deism"—the belief that faith is about doing good and being happy, and that God helps us feel good about ourselves.

This wasn't Lot's best decision, and we see the first hint of that in verse 13:

"Now the men of Sodom were evil, sinning greatly against the LORD."

Without seeking God for counsel, Lot looked toward Sodom and saw that it was good. That should sound familiar because it was the first mistake humanity ever made. Using their own wisdom, Adam and Eve looked toward the fruit God had told them not to eat and decided that it was good. Lot did the same thing.

The Scriptures say later that Lot actually ended up living in Sodom, not just near it. Over time the city drew him in, and before he knew it he was surrounded by everything that opposed the God he loved.

We experience this all the time. We want to know where the line is between "right" and "wrong" so we can get as close to it as possible without going over. We think we can enjoy ourselves more if we're closer to that line, and we're confident we'll never cross it.

But we always do.

In what areas do you regularly "walk the line" between God and the world?

What impact do these areas have on your walk with Christ?

As a pastor, I (Halim) get those questions all the time: How far is too far? When is it officially sex? Pornography is okay if I'm not cheating on my wife, right? What am I allowed to do as a Christian?

It's foolishness. If we keep trying to hug the line, we're going to cross the line. And we know it.

I know it. I remember making promises to God as a young man. I would tell Him to just let me live the way that I wanted to live—I'd study hard, get a good job, and make lots of money. Then I'd give lots of money to the church and be a good deacon or someone that helps with the offering at the very least. I remember telling God to wait while each day I tried to get as close to the line as possible.

 Leading a group? It's the way to go. Find extra questions and teaching tools in the leader kit, available at *threadsmedia.com/creationrestored.*

That's no way to live, and we need look no further than Lot's wife to see why:

> "The sun had risen over the land when Lot reached Zoar. Then out of the sky the LORD rained burning sulfur on Sodom and Gomorrah from the LORD. He demolished these cities, the entire plain, all the inhabitants of the cities, and whatever grew on the ground. But his wife looked back and became a pillar of salt" (Genesis 19:23-26).

I like what Tim Keller wrote about this moment:

> "The picture of Lot's wife reminds us that we cannot tell God, 'I'll flee to you when I'm ready.' It's typical, for example, for younger adults to want to postpone a strong spiritual commitment until they have 'experienced more of life.' But you don't know whether your heart will be too hard or indifferent to repent and turn to Him later. We must never put off submission to God whenever we sense Him calling to us in our hearts. If He is softening your heart and drawing you, you have no right to tell Him—'Come back and help me about five years from now.' You may find that you will spiritually harden— become stone."[1]

The Bible is clear: don't get as close to sin as you can. Get as close to Jesus as you can.

OUR ONLY HOPE

If we have the same problem as Lot, what can we do? In order to answer that question, we need to dig a little deeper into the core defects of Lot's heart—and all our hearts.

> "At daybreak the angels urged Lot on: 'Get up! Take your wife and your two daughters who are here, or you will be swept away in the punishment of the city.' But he hesitated. Because of the LORD's compassion for him, the men grabbed his hand, his wife's hand, and the hands of his two daughters. Then they brought him out and left him outside the city" (Genesis 19:15-16).

Lot's behavior in these verses is shocking. Just when the angels are about to annihilate the city completely, the Bible tells us that Lot "hesitated." In the original Hebrew language, that word means Lot "questioned and delayed." Take a minute to think about that:

- *When did Lot hesitate?* The morning Sodom was to be destroyed.
- *Where did he hesitate?* Within the walls of the city about to be decimated.
- *Before whom did he hesitate?* The angels sent to bring God's wrath on the city.

Doesn't that seem nuts? God's promise of judgment was so clear, so explicit, so imminent. And yet Lot hesitated. It seems absolutely incredible and unbelievable that he could make such a decision.

Of course, as J. C. Ryle pointed out, we do it all the time:

> "There are many Christian men and Christian women in this day very like Lot. . . . They believe in heaven, and yet seem faintly to long for it; and in hell, and yet seem little to fear it. They love the Lord Jesus; but the work they do for Him is small. They hate the devil; but they often appear to tempt him to come to them. They know the time is short; but they live as if it were long. They know they have a battle to fight; yet a man might think they were at peace. They know they have a race to run; yet they often look like people sitting still. They know the Judge is at the door, and there is wrath to come; and yet they appear half asleep. Astonishing they should be what they are, and yet be nothing more!"[2]

What's your reaction to those statements? Why?

I hope those words resonate with you; they sure describe me. In fact, they are me! I'm Lot. I know the truth of what the Bible says, and yet my heart hesitates and lingers.

So, is there any hope? As a matter of fact, there is—both for Lot and for us. We saw it when the angels "grabbed" Lot and his family and basically dragged them out of the city. Why did the angels do this? "Because of the LORD's compassion for him" (v. 16).

Understand what that means. The only reason someone like Lot could be saved—the only reason someone like you or me can be saved—is the mercy of the Lord.

Even as believers, our fundamental flaw is that we hesitate. We don't fully trust; we don't fully believe; and therefore we don't obey. We love God, but we also love the things of the world. We hate our sin, but we also love our sin.

When our day of judgment comes and we're in our beds, breathing our last, our only hope is that Jesus might set His compassion on us—that He would seize us by our hand and force us out of the way of the coming wrath of God by putting us outside of His judgment and into His mercy.

 A long-term research project conducted by the Barna Group revealed that more than two-thirds of Americans consider themselves "spiritual" or "religious," but only 18 percent claim to be "totally committed" to spiritual development.[3]

The stories in Genesis 18–19 say a lot about the process of our salvation:

- Sarah shows us that faith is birthed by God and demands our obedience.
- Abraham's pleading for Sodom and Gomorrah shows that God is willing to extend great grace by not punishing sin—if one can be found who is righteous. God is gracious to those who have no righteousness at all by being willing to count the righteousness of another as their own.
- Lot shows us that even with a faith birthed by God—one that demands faithful obedience—we still depend on God to create that obedience inside of us. We need Him to both start and finish the process.

Paul wrote about all of this in Philippians 1:6:

"I am sure of this, that He who started a good work in you will carry it on to completion until the day of Christ Jesus."

If you're starting to feel like the basis for salvation has nothing to do with us and our actions, you're right. In fact, that's our only hope.

Maybe that lack of control seems horrifying to you. Maybe it makes you feel dependent, not in charge. But trust me—it's ultimately a wonderful thing. If everything for our salvation rests in God's hands, and we're completely dependent upon Him and not ourselves, there is hope that we will actually be saved. Because He is faithful even when we are faithless. He birthed this great faith in us in the beginning, and He will be faithful to keep His promise to sustain that faith in us until the end.

What issues or temptations make you hesitate, like Lot?

Do you agree that a salvation that rests totally in God's hands is "ultimately a wonderful thing"? Why or why not?

LOVE GOD ABOVE ALL THINGS

One of the overarching themes of faith is that it directs the people of God to love Him above all else. Faith enables us to believe God in light of impossible circumstances, in cases of extreme hopelessness, and even when the core of our being starts believing that the world has better promises to offer.

 "The Lord is my rock, my fortress, and my deliverer, my God, my mountain where I seek refuge, my shield and the horn of my salvation, my stronghold" (Psalm 18:2).

Faith overcomes everything to train God's people to love Him chiefly. That's the idea behind the strange (even disturbing) story of Abraham and Isaac on Mount Moriah:

> **"After these things God tested Abraham and said to him, 'Abraham!'**
>
> **"'Here I am,' he answered.**
>
> **"'Take your son,' He said, 'your only son Isaac, whom you love, go to the land of Moriah, and offer him there as a burnt offering on one of the mountains I will tell you about'" (Genesis 22:1-2).**

Remember that God had promised to provide Abraham with a son. Isaac was the central promise that all of God's other promises hinged upon, not Ishmael. Isaac was everything. He was the culmination of what Abraham and Sarah had been wanting and seeking their entire lives.

But there's a danger in placing such a high value on anything other than God. Sometimes we focus on the promises of God and the things He has given so much that we end up clinging to those things even more tightly than we cling to Him. We start to love those things more than we love God. Consequently, our faith in God is no longer grounded in Him as a Person of inherent trustworthiness and value. Rather, it becomes centered on God giving us what we want.

When God commanded Abraham to bring Isaac up to the mountain and offer him as a sacrifice, it wasn't because God had decided to go back on His promise—it wasn't because God was cruel or vindictive. It was to test whether or not Abraham's affections were primarily for the Giver or the gift.

God demands exclusivity when it comes to our worth and love. He doesn't want to be on the same level as the things and people we love the most. He wants more. He demands a greater love than we could give to anything else because that's best for us—because He is our best source for happiness and joy:

> **"You reveal the path of life to me; in Your presence is abundant joy; in Your right hand are eternal pleasures" (Psalm 16:11).**

We've all experienced the failure of temporary joy, even if we don't realize it. Everything that has ever made us happy has eventually faded. People, places, status, excitement, wealth, power, comfort, even the latest electronic gizmo—they're all finite, flawed, and deteriorating. But not God.

....

 The "land of Moriah" was later renamed Jerusalem. It's where Jesus was crucified thousands of years after Isaac was spared.

Where do you usually run when you need "temporary joy"?

How long does it typically take you to become tired of whatever makes you happy?

We may find happiness in other things for a little while, but if we want to remain happy, joyful, and fulfilled forevermore, then the object of our happiness must be of infinite worth. The object of our happiness and joyfulness and fulfillment must be God.

And it can be.

It's because of God's great love that He creates faith in us. And it's because of God's great love that He promises to orchestrate our lives in such a way that our faith is increased, and we believe that He is better and higher than anything else—and thus the recipient of our greatest love and worship.

There will be times when we lose things that are precious to us. There will be times of suffering and pain. In those moments, our hearts will want to believe that God is not for us but against us and not keeping His promises. But we need to believe what is true. We need God to increase our faith so we can believe His promises are good.

God's promises were never meant to be the objects of our worship. They're meant to point us back to Him.

When we're most satisfied in God, when He's all our hope and stay, when we could lose everything else except Him and still say we have more than we ever knew possible—then we will see that the faith He created in us He has also grown and matured to make us truly love God above all else.

APPLY TO LIFE

As you read through the Bible this week, keep an eye out for any texts that contain promises from God. (Jesus' words in Matthew 11:28 are a good example: "Come to Me, all of you who are weary and burdened, and I will give you rest.") Use pages 50-51 to write down any promises you encounter. At the end of the week, write down how those promises impact your life.

In Genesis 19, the first 29 verses describe the destruction of Sodom and Gomorrah. This week, commit 29 minutes to praying through those verses—one minute for each verse. You don't need an agenda or structure for this kind of prayer. Simply meditate on each verse and listen to whatever the Holy Spirit may choose to say.

This session talked about loving God above all other things, but that can be hard to measure. One way to get a sense of your priorities is to look through your budget or bank statements from the past month. When you finish, answer the following questions:

1. What are the top five areas (house, car, food, entertainment, etc.) in which you've spent your money?
2. What do you find surprising about those five areas?
3. Which area would you most like to change? Why?

GOD'S LOVE CONQUERS SIN

GENESIS 25

SESSION THREE

"For this is the statement of the promise: At this time I will come, and Sarah will have a son. And not only that, but also Rebekah received a promise when she became pregnant by one man, our ancestor Isaac. For though her sons had not been born yet or done anything good or bad, so that God's purpose according to election might stand—not from works but from the One who calls—she was told: The older will serve the younger. As it is written: I have loved Jacob, but I have hated Esau" (Romans 9:9-13).

Here's a scary question: Could the fall happen more than once?

Through Abraham, we've seen that the only way to regain intimacy with God is through faith. More, we know that faith isn't something we can muster on our own. The kind of faith we see in Abraham, the saving kind, can only come through God's work—it's birthed through His Word and overcomes the void and darkness of our hearts, just like God spoke light into the darkness in Genesis 1.

So that's good news.

We've also seen that God was preserving a line of people for Himself through Abraham, Isaac, and Jacob. This line led to the fulfillment of His ultimate promise: the birth of Jesus. And just like Abraham demonstrated faith when he believed God would provide Isaac, his promised son, we experience salvation by placing our faith in the true promised Son, Jesus.

That's good news, too.

But the scary question is still out there: Once we're reconciled to God through faith, how do we know that we won't blow it again?

After all, when God gives us faith and reconciles us back to Him, He's basically fixing the problem that was created by Adam and Eve's original sin. God takes away our sin—He brings us to a righteous state—so that we can once again be in a relationship with Him.

But Adam and Eve were already in a sinless state when they sinned! Their hearts weren't bent away from God yet. They enjoyed a perfect relationship with Him. And yet in spite of that perfection, when they were given the choice between everything that was good and just one thing that was bad—they chose the bad.

And so will we.

If Adam and Eve chose sin over God in a sinless state, how much more will we choose sin over God in our sinful state? Even if we are reconciled back to God through faith, we still have a sinful nature at war with the Spirit of God inside of us. So how do we know that this time we'll stay reconciled and not fall all over again?

In many ways these issues boil down to two realities that threaten our eternal security once we're reconciled back to God through faith:

- *The evil within:* What can we do about our own sinful nature and tendency to sin?
- *The evil without:* What about the depravity of the world that seeks to destroy us?

 Listen to "Long Road (to Nowhere)" by Eric Peters from the *Creation Restored* playlist, available at *threadsmedia.com/creationrestored.*

Those are questions we'll be addressing in the pages to come. To do so, we'll focus on the lives of the two remaining central characters in Genesis: Jacob (the evil within) and Joseph (the evil without).

To start, we'll turn to Jacob and seek to understand how God will handle the problem of sin that still remains after we trust Him in faith, as Abraham did.

JACOB HAVE I LOVED

Fast-forward to Genesis 25, and you'll notice quite a few changes in the family of promise. Abraham died, and Isaac took a wife named Rebekah. Like Isaac's mother (before God intervened), Rebekah was barren. So Isaac went before the Lord and asked Him to open her womb.

God's response was interesting:

> "Isaac prayed to the LORD on behalf of his wife because she was childless. The LORD heard his prayer, and his wife Rebekah conceived. But the children inside her struggled with each other, and she said, 'Why is this happening to me?' So she went to inquire of the LORD.
>
> "And the LORD said to her: two nations are in your womb; two people will come from you and be separated. One people will be stronger than the other, and the older will serve the younger" (Genesis 25:21-23).

Several things stand out from these verses. First, God responded to Isaac's prayer by providing not one, but two children for his wife. Second, the twins "struggled" together inside of Rebekah's womb. In the Hebrew that word literally means to "smash" or "crush"; it's a word that conveys destruction. (If you're imagining a scene from the *Alien* movies, that's kind of the idea). It's not surprising, then, that Rebekah cried out to God.

The Lord graciously answered her cry with an explanation. The struggle inside of her was a picture of two nations that would emerge from the lineages of her children. These nations would be divided and separate.

Then God dropped the bombshell: "The older will serve the younger."

That's a shocking statement, but it can easily be lost in translation for those of us raised in a present-day western culture. In virtually all patriarchal societies, the elder son was honored more highly than the younger sons; he was given the lion's share of the inheritance and was the head of the family when the father died.

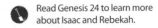

Read Genesis 24 to learn more about Isaac and Rebekah.

From the world's perspective, the older son was the "chosen one" on behalf of the family. The very nature of being oldest commanded power, status, and certain rights of entitlement.

God's declaration to Rebekah flew in the face of those expectations. He reversed the natural hierarchy. Of course, from earlier chapters in Genesis we know this isn't the first time God chose the second-born child over the first. Remember that Ishmael was also passed over as the child of promise—God chose Isaac, the second-born, to be the son through whom He would bring about the Messiah.

Clearly, God's economy is different than the world's. While the world lifts up those who are strong, competent, and privileged to receive blessings, God looks to the periphery of society, the dismissed, and gathers them for His blessings. He takes the weak, forgotten, and estranged and sets His love upon them—He lifts them up and seals them with a promise of His covenant, something far greater than the world could ever offer or withhold.

The E-Word

God chose Jacob to continue the line of salvation, and He passed over Esau. That choice had significant consequences for Isaac's family, certainly, but things didn't stop there. In fact, we still feel the ramifications of that choice today.

Look at what the apostle Paul had to say in his New Testament letter to the church at Rome:

> "But it is not as though the word of God has failed. For not all who are descended from Israel are Israel. Neither are they all children because they are Abraham's descendants. On the contrary, your offspring will be traced through Isaac. That is, it is not the children by physical descent who are God's children, but the children of the promise are considered to be the offspring.
>
> "For this is the statement of the promise: 'At this time I will come, and Sarah will have a son.' And not only that, but also Rebekah received a promise when she became pregnant by one man, our ancestor Isaac. For though her sons had not been born yet or done anything good or bad, so that God's purpose according to election might stand—not from works but from the One who calls—she was told: 'The older will serve the younger.'
>
> "As it is written: 'I have loved Jacob, but I have hated Esau'" (Romans 9:6-13).

What does it mean that God "hated" Esau?

To study more about the doctrine of election, check out *Election and Predestination*, by Paul Jewett, and *The Cross and Salvation* (chapter 3), by Bruce Demarest.

How do you react to the idea of God hating someone?

Paul explained to the Romans how God fulfilled the promise of the Abrahamic covenant despite the fact that many Israelites had rejected the Messiah. Many people thought that anyone who came through the physical lineage of Abraham, any descendent of his, was guaranteed salvation. They believed this great gift came through the family you were born into—that God owed salvation as a birthright to anyone who qualified as an ethnic Jew.

Paul used the story of Jacob and Esau to blow that argument out of the water.

Actually, he started by reminding the audience that the promise came through Isaac's birth, not through Ishmael, who was also born from Abraham's seed. Then Paul extended the point by explaining that before Jacob and Esau were born, before they had done anything good or bad, God chose Jacob for salvation.

More, Paul answered the "why" question. He gave us the reason why God wanted the older to serve the younger:

> **"For though her sons had not been born yet or done anything good or bad, so that God's purpose according to election might stand—not from works but from the One who calls—she was told: 'The older will serve the younger'"** (vv. 11-12, emphasis added).

Paul wanted the Romans to know—God wants me and you to know—that it was because of His electing purpose, not any human merit, that God determined Esau would serve Jacob. It was strictly because of the call of God that Jacob received salvation through the promise and Esau didn't.

That's a controversial word: "election." As we'll see, it makes some people uncomfortable, and that may be the case for you. But it's vital that we understand the doctrine of election if we want to properly understand the story of Jacob and Esau.

If He Has Set His Love on Us . . .
Let's not sugarcoat anything here; this is a challenging truth. Paul claimed that no amount of good deeds can connect people to God if they haven't been called by Him. And there are people who haven't been called.

There are Esaus even today.

 "There is no more humbling doctrine in Scripture than that of election, none that promotes more gratitude, and, consequently, none more sanctifying. Believers should not be afraid of it, but rejoice in it with adoration." —Charles Spurgeon[1]

But Paul's words should also be a source of great hope, because no depth of sin will keep us from God if He has set His love on us.

This can be a hard reality to stomach. And yet the alternative implications of a salvation based on our merit or performance are far more horrific. We've seen time and time again how naturally failure and unbelief come to human beings. Even with the capacity for faith birthed in us by God, we still don't choose His ways over our own every single time. We still fall short.

God doesn't.

The unconditional election of God, solely rooted in His freedom to choose, is the only type of love that will keep us secure forever. If His election is somehow conditioned on us— conditioned on our ability to obey and be "good"—then we could actually cause God to not love us anymore. Have you ever considered that? If we are the determining factor for salvation, then we must be immovable in our faith 100 percent of the time. But because God's election is unconditional, not conditioned upon our good or bad, we can be secure in His love because He is unchanging. He is the same yesterday, today, and forever.

According to the Bible, I (Halim) was dead in my transgression and sin, incapable of choosing God on my own or making my own way back to heaven. But because God chose me before the foundation of the world, because He set His love on me, He grabbed a hold of me and gave me life. And now I can have days where I am holding onto Him, too—where I am submitting to Him with everything I have. Since He grabbed me first and is holding me based on His electing purpose, I can be firmly in His grip even when I let go of Him and try to go my own way. His grip secures me, which means that no one, not even myself, can snatch me out of His hand.

Ultimately, the final security of my salvation isn't based on my choice to hold onto God but on His choice to hold onto me. It isn't based on the strength of my grip but on the strength of His.

Do you agree or disagree that the concept of election is encouraging? Why?

We see this concept clearly illustrated through the life of Jacob. God set His love on Jacob, and despite the wishes of others—not to mention Jacob's efforts to flail around and get away—God didn't let him go.

 Watch the *Creation Restored* video
"God's Love Conquers Sin," available
at *threadsmedia.com/creationrestored*.

GOD'S WILL OVERCOMES

Let's fast-forward from the birth of Esau and Jacob to a couple events that happened after they became adults. The first involves a birthright and a bowl of soup:

> "Once when Jacob was cooking a stew, Esau came in from the field exhausted. He said to Jacob, 'Let me eat some of that red stuff, because I'm exhausted.' That is why he was also named Edom.
>
> "Jacob replied, 'First sell me your birthright.'
>
> "'Look,' said Esau, 'I'm about to die, so what good is a birthright to me?'
>
> "Jacob said, 'Swear to me first.' So he swore to Jacob and sold his birthright to him. Then Jacob gave bread and lentil stew to Esau; he ate, drank, got up, and went away. So Esau despised his birthright" (Genesis 25:29-34).

That's a familiar story, but we should still be shocked when we read it. The "birthright" mentioned here referred to the lion's share of the inheritance and future leadership of the family. How could someone trade it for a bowl of soup? That's ridiculous! Nobody but Esau would be foolish enough to do something like that—right?

Let's look at the second event:

> "When Isaac was old and his eyes were so weak that he could not see, he called his older son Esau and said to him, 'My son.'
>
> "And he answered, 'Here I am.'
>
> "He said, 'Look, I am old and do not know the day of my death. Take your hunting gear, your quiver and bow, and go out in the field to hunt some game for me. Then make me a delicious meal that I love and bring it to me to eat, so that I can bless you before I die'" (Genesis 27:1-4).

That may seem simple, but there's a big problem with Isaac's instructions. It was customary to call all of the sons together when a patriarch was on his deathbed, but in this case Isaac secretly called Esau in order to bless him alone. Isaac almost certainly knew what God had declared to Rebekah—he was aware God had chosen Jacob as the promised son to bear the messianic seed and continue the lineage leading to Jesus. He also knew that Esau had already sold his birthright to Jacob for a bowl of soup.

 Deuteronomy 21:15-17 contains specific instructions for firstborn sons, unloved wives, and more.

All of this affirms that Jacob should have been the uncontested recipient of the highest blessing from Isaac. But there was another factor behind Isaac's actions:

> **"Isaac loved Esau because he had a taste for wild game, but Rebekah loved Jacob" (Genesis 25:28).**

Esau was Isaac's favorite for no better reason than Esau's ability to kill wild animals and cook a tasty meal. And that's what Isaac had in mind when he was ready to give out his blessing. He commanded Esau to go out into the field and hunt, so he could bring Isaac a savory meal and receive his blessing as the firstborn.

Think about that. We denounce Esau (and rightfully so) for giving up his birthright for something as insignificant as a bowl of soup. But Isaac was willing to go against the will of God—willing to commit an enduring sin by blessing Esau instead of Jacob, thus directly disobeying God—in exchange for a savory meal.

Do you find Esau and Isaac's perspectives hard to understand? Do you look down on them? Do you wonder how they could be so blind to the lunacy of their actions?

You and I do the same thing every time we sin.

When God declares that our affections shouldn't go out to certain things, if we grab them anyway then we're exchanging obedience to the Father, which is exceedingly valuable, for something temporary. We trade eternal rewards for instant gratification. Sin tries to rip us off, and the sad thing is we almost never see the truth until we've already made the trade.

What are the "bowl of soup" temptations that you regularly reach for?

Where have you had victory in the past over those sins?

Back to Esau and Jacob. Their mother, Rebekah, overheard Isaac's plan, and she immediately set in motion a counterplot to ensure that her favorite son, Jacob, received the blessing instead of his brother. She made the delicious dinner her husband wanted and sent Jacob into Isaac's room wearing Esau's clothes. She also put goats' hair on Jacob's arms and the back of his neck to make sure her husband would be deceived.

 "And make sure that there isn't any immoral or irreverent person like Esau, who sold his birthright in exchange for one meal. For you know that later, when he wanted to inherit the blessing, he was rejected because he didn't find any opportunity for repentance, though he sought it with tears" (Hebrews 12:16-17).

SESSION THREE CREATION RESTORED

Rebekah's plan worked, and Isaac gave his blessing to Jacob, thinking he was giving it to Esau:

> **"Then his father Isaac said to him, 'Please come closer and kiss me, my son.' So he came closer and kissed him. When Isaac smelled his clothes, he blessed him and said:**
>
> **"'Ah, the smell of my son is like the smell of a field that the LORD has blessed. May God give to you—from the dew of the sky and from the richness of the land—an abundance of grain and new wine. May peoples serve you and nations bow down to you. Be master over your brothers; may your mother's sons bow down to you. Those who curse you will be cursed, and those who bless you will be blessed'" (Genesis 27:26-29).**

Notice that, even with all the preparations, it took a while for Isaac to become fully convinced. He wanted to feel Jacob to see if he was hairy like Esau. He wanted to taste the food to confirm whether it was the kind Esau would prepare. He even asked for a kiss so that he could determine if this person had the smell of Esau. In other words, Isaac used all of his earthly faculties, all of his senses—sight, hearing, touch, taste, and smell—to ensure that his blessing was going to his chosen son, Esau, and not the son God had chosen. He did everything he could think of to consciously fight against the will of God.

In the end, however, the will of God prevailed. As it always does.

In case you're wondering, Jacob wasn't innocent in this whole affair—not by a long shot. He was prepared to wrangle away his brother's birthright with a bowl of soup, and he was equally ready and willing to steal the blessing through another meal. In many ways, his career as a liar and manipulator was just getting started.

What we're going to see next is that the only possible reason someone like Jacob could be saved is because the sovereign will of God can't be thwarted by sin or anything else. Through Jacob's story, God shows us that our sins, no matter how numerous, can't threaten His plan to save us.

SINS AND LONGINGS

Here's an interesting question: What was Jacob's predominant sin? Anyone reading the text can see he was a liar, thief, and manipulator—just to name a few of the marks against him. But what was the deep, internal longing that produced all those sinful actions? What was underneath, waging war in his heart?

I think we can infer from what we've seen of Jacob that he had a significant, powerful longing for approval. He wanted to be blessed and accepted by someone, and it started with his father. Throughout his entire life, Jacob had seen his father favor Esau over him. Even on his deathbed, Isaac wanted to bless Esau over Jacob—and he was willing to disobey God in order to make it happen.

Yes, God chose Jacob, but that truth seems to have impacted him less than knowing his earthly father chose someone else.

Jacob's longing for approval extended even beyond his father as time passed. He spent much of his life trying to find acceptance from Isaac, from his mother, from Esau, from Laban (as we'll see later), and from his wife. He was so desperate for affection, he was willing to lie, cheat, and steal to get it.

These longings aren't limited to Jacob, nor are they evil in and of themselves. We all have a deep desire to be truly known and fully approved. Jacob gives us a frightening picture of how far we'll go to get it.

Where do you see the desire for approval reflected in today's culture?

In what way is the desire for approval reflected in your life?

A Bad Solution

Faced with the prospect of never having his father's approval, Jacob decided he needed to be someone else. Jacob didn't look right, sound right, or smell right. He wasn't manly enough or athletic enough. He wasn't all of the things he knew his dad wanted him to be, so he dressed up as someone else in order to receive what he could never get as himself.

When Jacob went into his father's room under the disguise of everything Esau, he was better positioned than ever before to finally get what he'd been looking for. When he leaned in close to his dad, he finally saw that look he'd always dreamed of—a joyful, proud smile.

But as he listened to his father's blessing spoken over him, do you think it felt as good as he'd always imagined it would? Do you think it quenched his deep thirst for approval?

....

 According to a 2010 report by the Pew Research Center, 27 percent of children in the U.S. live apart from their fathers.[2]

I don't. I think the experience was bittersweet because his father wasn't giving anything to him—not really. His father still believed he was blessing Esau. Though Jacob looked and smelled and felt like Esau on the outside, he was still Jacob on the inside. No amount of trickery or deceit could change that.

As a result, Jacob spent the next phase of his life grabbing for the same thing in the same way: deceiving and stealing as much as he had to in order to feel like he mattered.

A Better Solution

Years later, something miraculous happened to Jacob in connection with his search for approval. He'd been banished from his family for 20 years because of his schemes and deceptions, but he was on his way back home. On the journey, he had an encounter with a mysterious man who we'd considered strange by any account:

> **"Jacob was left alone, and a man wrestled with him until daybreak. When the man saw that He could not defeat him, He struck Jacob's hip socket as they wrestled and dislocated his hip. Then He said to Jacob, 'Let Me go, for it is daybreak.'**
>
> **"But Jacob said, 'I will not let You go unless You bless me'"** (Genesis 32:24-26).

Weird, right? But later in the text we read that the mysterious man wasn't really a man at all. It was God. Jacob was literally, physically struggling with God. Once he realized what was going on, he stopped trying to get away from the man and instead clung to Him.

Did you catch what Jacob said? "I will not let You go unless You bless me."

For decades, Jacob had been looking for approval from the wrong father. He'd been searching for acceptance and admiration in all the wrong places, not realizing that he already possessed the very thing he wanted so desperately: the love of his Heavenly Father.

Before Jacob was born, before he'd done anything to earn it or lose it, God set His electing love on Jacob and fully approved of him. It wasn't because of Jacob's merit, but by God's sovereign choice. Jacob had been running around looking everywhere to find what was already his in infinite measure.

Remember when Jacob dressed up as Esau in order to steal his father's blessing? That's a poignant picture, and it foreshadows an opportunity that we have been given because of the promised Messiah who was born from Jacob's line.

 Leading a group? It's the way to go. Find extra questions and teaching tools in the leader kit, available at *threadsmedia.com/creationrestored.*

The Bible tells us Jesus is the firstborn among many brethren; He's our true older brother. Look what Paul has to say in Galatians:

> **"For as many of you as have been baptized into Christ have put on Christ like a garment" (3:27).**

Jacob putting on Esau's clothes was a feeble attempt at changing who he was and becoming someone better. However, those clothes only changed him on the outside. But his actions point us to Jesus and our opportunity to "put on Christ like a garment." The great news is that this garment changes us from the inside out to the point where we actually do become better people. We become like Jesus.

Because of Christ's clothing we're no longer thieves and liars; we become the rightful heirs of God's blessing. His covering makes us authentic heirs, not imposters. In other words, Jesus put on our clothes (humanity) and died as a sinner would so that we could put on His clothes (righteousness) and live as the approved children of God.

JACOB'S DREAM

As you can imagine, Jacob's scheme didn't go over too well with Esau, and the text tells us Esau actually planned to kill his brother after his father died and the time for mourning had passed. Rebekah found out about this scheme, and she came up with another plan. She convinced Isaac to send Jacob to Paddan-aram, where Rebekah grew up, so that he could find a wife among their people.

We catch up with Jacob in the wilderness, on the run, fleeing for his life from his own home. After all the scheming and deceiving and orchestrating, the text picks up his story again as he lies on the desert floor using a hard stone for a pillow—homeless, hunted, and alone.

That's when he met God for the first time:

> **"And he dreamed: A stairway was set on the ground with its top reaching heaven, and God's angels were going up and down on it. Yahweh was standing there beside him, saying, 'I am Yahweh, the God of your father Abraham and the God of Isaac. I will give you and your offspring the land that you are now sleeping on. Your offspring will be like the dust of the earth, and you will spread out toward the west, the east, the north, and the south. All the peoples on earth will be blessed through you and your offspring. Look, I am with you and will watch over you wherever you go. I will bring you back to this land, for I will not leave you until I have done what I have promised you'" (Genesis 28:12-15).**

 Jacob's journey from Beer-sheba to Haran was about 500 miles.

After all the deceptive, manipulative things Jacob had done to get what he wanted, God came to him. Jacob didn't go looking for God; the Lord sought him out. Still, I would've expected God to bring the heat just a little bit. There was no shortage of sin to address in our friend Jacob. But God didn't speak with judgment or harshness. Instead, God spoke to Jacob in a way that was both specific and intimate. And it changed his life.

First, God reminded Jacob that He was the Lord of Jacob's grandfather and father. This is the God Jacob had only encountered verbally from stories passed down through his ancestors. Before that day, Jacob had never personally encountered God.

Second, God made several promises of blessing to Jacob. These started out as the same promises given to his father, Isaac. Blessings of land and offspring were reinforced—including the messianic prophecy that "all the peoples on earth will be blessed through you."

Notice how God used these promises to address Jacob's immediate needs. He'd been cast out of his home without any possessions or a place to live, so God promised him land and a place he could call home. Esau planned to kill Jacob, so God promised him protection.

But then God told Jacob something he desperately needed to hear: "I am with you." God promised Jacob He wouldn't leave until He'd done what He promised. That's the promise that touched the deepest need of Jacob's heart, and all of a sudden Jacob decided to set up a pillar of remembrance at Bethel. He immediately began worshiping God. This was the first time we see Jacob seek to honor someone outside of himself.

Which of those promises speaks to you most right now?

Which of God's promises are you currently counting on and hoping for?

Here's the bad news: Jacob was about to enter a time of difficulty and discipline in Paddan-aram. That season contained events and circumstances that would make it easy to doubt the blessings God had just spoken to him, and the implications of those events would last Jacob's entire lifetime. In order to make it through, Jacob would have to trust that God was telling the truth.

It's ironic. God chose to mature Jacob the deceiver by making him trust a promise.

A WIFE AT THE WELL—AGAIN

Jacob continued his journey east and arrived at a well where many shepherds prepared to water their flocks. Those shepherds knew Jacob's uncle Laban, the brother of his mother, Rebekah. While they talked, a young girl emerged with her flocks and approached the well for water.

What happened next was romantic stuff:

> **"While he was still speaking with them, Rachel came with her father's sheep, for she was a shepherdess. As soon as Jacob saw his uncle Laban's daughter Rachel with his sheep, he went up and rolled the stone from the opening and watered his uncle Laban's sheep. Then Jacob kissed Rachel and wept loudly. He told Rachel that he was her father's relative, Rebekah's son. She ran and told her father"** (Genesis 29:9-12).

Guys, you know exactly what was happening there, right? The shepherds were waiting for enough men to arrive so they could roll away the stone together and water their sheep (vv. 1–3). But as soon as Rachel hit the scene, Jacob ran up to the heavy stone and heaved it out of the way all by himself. Hiyah!

We can imagine what was going through Jacob's mind. He knew the story of how his father and mother met. He was aware that Abraham's servant had met Rebekah at a well in Paddan-aram—possibly even the same well where he first saw Rachel. He must have been thinking: *Is God doing it again? Is He providing this beautiful woman for me just as He did for my father?*

Keep in mind, Jacob's uncle Laban, Rachel's father, was there when Abraham's servant showed up to take Rebekah back to marry Isaac. The servant came with loads of wealth to show that Rebekah would be well taken care of by her new husband. Laban knew the drill.

Yet Jacob arrived at his door with nothing but the clothes on his back. Laban must have wondered what was going on, but it was instantly obvious that Jacob was vulnerable—something Laban could take advantage of. That's right: Jacob didn't realize it at the time, but he had fallen in with someone even more devious and adept at scheming than himself.

What happened next is a well-known story. Jacob fell in love with Rachel and offered to work seven years for Laban in order to receive her as his wife. That was an exaggerated amount of time, by the way—a bride price far above what was expected. That's one of the ways the text makes it clear that Jacob was genuinely and passionately in love with Rachel.

Of course, that made what happened next all the more painful.

The Scriptures say those seven years "seemed like only a few days to him because of his love for her" (v. 20), and soon Jacob was ready to claim his bride. This was supposed to be the best day of his life—the moment he'd anticipated and dreamed about for seven years. Every day that passed during his labor was bearable because of the promise that he would receive Rachel as his wife.

But Laban had another idea:

> "Then Jacob said to Laban, 'Give me my wife, for my time is completed. I want to sleep with her.' So Laban invited all the men of the place to a feast. That evening, Laban took his daughter Leah and gave her to Jacob, and he slept with her. And Laban gave his slave Zilpah to his daughter Leah as her slave. When morning came, there was Leah! So he said to Laban, 'What is this you have done to me? Wasn't it for Rachel that I worked for you? Why have you deceived me?'" (Genesis 29:23-25).

Leah was Rachel's older sister, and the text says she "had ordinary eyes," which means she wasn't much to look at. But the main reason Jacob was upset (and rightfully so) was that she wasn't Rachel. She wasn't his beloved!

Even if you haven't been on Team Jacob so far in Genesis, you have to sympathize with him in that moment. Everything he'd planned and envisioned for his wedding night was ruined by Laban's deception. Why would his father-in-law do such a thing?

Laban's explanation is as sharp as a knife:

> "Laban answered, 'It is not the custom *in this place* to give the younger daughter in marriage before the firstborn. Complete this week of wedding celebration, and we will also give you this younger one in return for working yet another seven years for me'" (Genesis 29:26-27, emphasis added).

Burn. It's as if Laban said, "Maybe in Canaan you put the younger sibling ahead of the older, but that's not how we do things here." Translation: Laban knew what had happened between Jacob and Esau, and he was using that knowledge to send Jacob a message—and to wrangle from him another seven years of work.

Again, the situation dripped with irony.

 "The elders and all the people who were at the gate said, 'We are witnesses. May the Lord make the woman who is entering your house like Rachel and Leah, who together built the house of Israel'" (Ruth 4:11).

In order to get the family blessing, Jacob had deceived Isaac by pretending to be the older brother when he was actually the younger. On his wedding night, Laban inverted Jacob's scheme by disguising the older sister to deceive Jacob into thinking she was the younger.

In other words, God was giving Jacob a taste of his own medicine. And he knew it.

That's why you don't see Jacob throw a fit or demand that Rachel be given to him immediately. He knew this discipline was for him. He knew the tables had turned because of the consequences of his own sin. This was no coincidence.

So Jacob committed to serving another seven years under a man who was an even greater cheat than himself. In doing so, he got Rachel as his wife—and a lot more. He also got a lifelong opportunity to watch the consequences of his sin play out in his life, and in the lives of the people he loved.

DISCIPLINE AND LOVE

As Jacob slogged away for another seven years, do you think he started to wonder about the promises God had spoken to him in the desert? After all, God said He would be with Jacob and keep him wherever he went. Shouldn't God have thwarted Laban's plan to sabotage Jacob's life and marriage? Why didn't He intervene and save Jacob from that pain?

Up to that point, God had demonstrated grace upon grace to Jacob by sparing him from the consequences of his sin and blessing him despite his many failures. Now God demonstrated His grace in a different way. God let Jacob experience some of those consequences, but not for the purpose of punishing him; rather, it was for the purpose of loving him.

God used the pain and suffering that followed Jacob's failure in order to root out sin in his life and mature him into a man of God.

I don't know about you, but I've often wondered why God insists on doing things that way. Why doesn't He just make us holy immediately after we become Christians? Why do we have to suffer through sinning and its consequences, like Jacob?

To wrap your head around those questions, imagine you're a kid helping your mom and dad around the house. Pretend your dad wants you to clean all the leaves off the front lawn. You could rake all the leaves into one pile and then throw them away all at once. But what if your dad took away the rake and told you to pick up each leaf individually and take them out to the trash can one at a time?

Here's the rub: Both methods of leaf-removal will result in a clean yard. But only the second approach will result in you hating the leaves.

That's why God addresses our sins over longer periods of time. As we grapple with our sin year after year, we start seeing it for what it really is: a deeply rooted, far-reaching problem. Wrestling with sin over time makes us view it as an enemy. If God snapped His fingers and removed sin all at once, we'd hardly notice it.

God wants us to feel the same way about our sin that He does. He wants us to reflect His heart in two ways: by being holy and by hating our sin. As the writer of Hebrews says, such growth in godliness often happens through discipline:

> **"Endure suffering as discipline: God is dealing with you as sons. For what son is there that a father does not discipline? But if you are without discipline—which all receive—then you are illegitimate children and not sons" (Hebrews 12:7-8).**

One of the biggest misconceptions about election is that once God sets His love on us, it doesn't matter what we do. Some believe God's electing love presents opportunity for immorality. But that isn't the picture we see of God in the Bible.

Because God loved Jacob—because He loves you and me—He will change us. He will craft our character. He will make us like Him. He will discipline us, and through that discipline we'll endure.

Because He set His love on us before the foundation of the world, He loves us in the midst of our sin; but because He loves us, He won't let us stay in our sin. His love will overwhelm our sin and we'll be different—we'll be like Him.

APPLY TO LIFE

Using pages 70-71, write down everything you know about the doctrine of election. Then ask yourself these questions:

1.   Am I comfortable or uncomfortable with the doctrine of election? Why?
2.   Do I agree or disagree with the doctrine of election? Why?

One day this week, pick out your grungiest set of clothes and wear them wherever you go—work, school, restaurants, etc. When someone mentions what you've got on, take a minute to silently confess to God that you are sinful, and that all of those righteous things you try to do are like filthy rags in His presence (Isaiah 64:6). The next day, wear your best outfit wherever you go. When someone mentions your clothes, take a minute to silently thank God that He has allowed you to "put on Christ like a garment" (Galatians 3:27).

GOD'S LOVE
GOES FURTHER

GENESIS 31–35

SESSION FOUR

"Jacob was left alone, and a man wrestled with him until daybreak. When the man saw that He could not defeat him, He struck Jacob's hip socket as they wrestled and dislocated his hip. Then He said to Jacob, 'Let Me go, for it is daybreak.' But Jacob said, 'I will not let You go unless You bless me'" (Genesis 32:24-26).

William Cowper was born in 1731, and he lived a fairly uneventful life—at least on the outside. On the inside, his life was a constant battle.

When he was 21, he became trapped in a deep, desperate depression. The darkness was so complete, he didn't believe he could fight his way through it. He wrote: "Day and night I was upon the rack, lying down in horror, and rising up in despair."

This wasn't slight unhappiness or doubt. This was such deep misery and anguish in his soul that each moment brought the challenge of breathing in and out. He experienced moments of relief over the years—times when he thought things might turn out OK. But each time the depression came crashing back once again.

When he was 32, Cowper took steps to end his life. He tried to drown, poison, and hang himself. In each separate attempt, he was interrupted and unsuccessful. Overwhelmed with guilt and shame, he began to lose his mind. Later that year, he was committed to an insane asylum.

In that unlikely place, his despair and agony were interrupted by the same great and glorious news that has interrupted so many of our lives. After six months in the asylum he found a Bible on a bench and opened it. He read about God's kindness and then turned to Romans 3:25 and read of the promise of Christ's redemption.

Later, he wrote:

> "Immediately I received the strength to believe it, and the full beams of the Sun of Righteousness shone upon me. I saw the sufficiency of the atonement He had made, my pardon sealed in His blood, and all the fullness and completeness of His justification. In a moment I believed, and received the gospel. . . . Unless the Almighty arm had been under me, I think I should have died with gratitude and joy. My eyes filled with tears, and my voice choked with transport; I could only look up to heaven in silent fear, overwhelmed with love and wonder."[1]

God met Cowper in the darkness and overwhelmed him with a love so great it shed light into the darkest of hearts and produced joy in the heart of a man destined for sorrow.

I (Matt) love hearing stories like that. They make much of God's redemptive power and His ability to save us and change us. But that wasn't the end of William Cowper's story.

....

Listen to "Beautiful, Beautiful"
by Francesca Battistelli from the
Creation Restored playlist, available at
threadsmedia.com/creationrestored.

SESSION FOUR CREATION RESTORED

I wish I could tell you that after such a powerful experience Cowper lived happily ever after, but that isn't the way God wrote his story. He continued to struggle with deep depression for the rest of his life. He continued to try unsuccessfully to commit suicide. He finally died in 1800 after telling his doctor that he felt "unutterable despair."

Cowper never conquered his battle with depression. He fought, but he never won.

Most of us would rather not know that part of the story. It makes us uncomfortable and unsure. We want to get brought up from the dirt, saved, and changed, and we want the next line of our testimonies to be: "They lived happily ever after."

But what happens when we find ourselves in the dirt once again? Did God fail us? Was the Romans 3:25 moment unreal? What happens if we wake up tomorrow and find our illness has returned or we're back in the dark past we fled so long ago? Will our hope remain if it's grounded in a past moment or encounter?

What are some of your favorite "happily ever after" stories?

Which biblical characters had a story similar to William Cowper's?

God takes broken people and puts them back together. He changes lives, heals addictions, and sets us free from eating disorders, sexual sin, and much more. He loves us enough to change us in the midst of all that. The gospel is powerful enough to impact people in a single moment and change their lives.

That kind of gospel hope doesn't end there, though. No one who is breathing air is finished with sin. No one whose heart is beating lives "happily ever after"—not yet. We need a gospel that will save us not just for a moment but for the rest of our lives.

In Genesis 31, we come to a perfect stopping point for Jacob's story. We see the "happily ever after" moment. Jacob's heart had been changed, his relationship with God had been redeemed, and his relationships with others had been restored. Unfortunately, the author of the text missed his chance to neatly wrap up the story.

 William Cowper was a famous poet in his day. He also wrote a number of hymns, including "There Is a Fountain Filled with Blood."

JACOB HAD CHANGED

Jacob endured several years on a bumpy road. His deceptions wrought more deception. With each attempt to trick and manipulate, Jacob found himself tricked and manipulated in turn. Yet in spite of Jacob's failure and disobedience, God reached into his life and set His favor upon him. God set his love on Jacob in the form of great and precious promises.

Reconnecting with Jacob in Genesis 31, it's clear that those promises had their intended effect. Jacob was changed:

> "Then the LORD said to him, 'Go back to the land of your fathers and to your family, and I will be with you.'

> "Jacob had Rachel and Leah called to the field where his flocks were. He said to them, 'I can see from your father's face that his attitude toward me is not the same, but the God of my father has been with me. You know that I've worked hard for your father and that he has cheated me and changed my wages 10 times. But God has not let him harm me. If he said, "The spotted sheep will be your wages," then all the sheep were born spotted. If he said, "The streaked sheep will be your wages," then all the sheep were born streaked. God has taken away your father's herds and given them to me.

> "'When the flocks were breeding, I saw in a dream that the streaked, spotted, and speckled males were mating with the females. In that dream the Angel of God said to me, "Jacob!" and I said, "Here I am." And He said, "Look up and see: all the males that are mating with the flocks are streaked, spotted, and speckled, for I have seen all that Laban has been doing to you. I am the God of Bethel, where you poured oil on the stone marker and made a solemn vow to Me. Get up, leave this land, and return to your native land"'" (vv. 3-13).

Let's explore in greater detail some of the ways Jacob had changed.

Jacob Had New Motives

Jacob had been working for his uncle for a long time, and wanting to leave wasn't a new feeling. He'd communicated his desire over and over again, but each time Laban had bribed him into staying.

After 20 years, what finally caused Jacob to leave wasn't another fight with Laban or the promise of wealth elsewhere. No, Jacob's mind was finally settled because God came to him and called him to return to his homeland.

 Read Genesis 29:31–30:43 to learn how Jacob's family and property were dramatically increased.

When Jacob heard that call, he didn't try to negotiate new terms with Laban. He didn't consider his options and discuss it with those around him. He didn't weigh the pros and cons. Jacob gathered up his family and gave them a speech sharing all that God had done and the call God had made on his life. Just like his grandfather Abraham, Jacob responded in obedience without hesitation.

This was new for him. All his life, Jacob had struggled with deceitfulness. At the heart of his deceitfulness was a deep fear that God wouldn't provide. Jacob had spent all his life managing fear, anxiety, and worry by planning and working to provide for himself. He'd used deceptions, lies, and tricks in order to get what he wanted. But now, for the first time, we see him make a decision based not on his own desires or gain, but out of love for God. Why? Because his motives had changed; he'd come to trust God.

Where do you see Jacob's motivations reflected in today's culture?

Jacob Decided to Trust God

In the speech Jacob gave to Rachel and Leah, he recapped God's faithfulness to them. He recounted Laban's attempts to steal from him, and how those attempts had failed in the hands of a faithful God. He reminded them of God's promise to be with him, and he told how this same God who had provided, protected, and led him all the way was commanding him to return home.

Jacob had finally learned to trust in God.

Indeed, the entire speech was a worshipful recounting of everything God had done. Jacob was finally starting to believe that God would provide for him, and it freed him from his usual anxiety and deceit. It even freed him enough to give God the glory.

In what situations do you find it most difficult to trust God?

Jacob Gave the Glory to God

After Jacob married Rachel, he agreed to work for Laban in return for a portion of his sheep. Genesis 30 tells how Jacob strategized and deceived to gain the larger portion of the animals. His scheme revolved around setting speckled branches near mating sheep in order to produce speckled lambs. That's something we view as ridiculous today given our scientific knowledge, but Jacob thought it was working at the time.

 During a 2006 study by the Pew Research Center, only 45 percent of respondents agreed that "most people can be trusted."[2]

His attitude changed in Genesis 31. When Jacob recounted how he gained all his flocks, he never mentioned his complex plans. Instead, he acknowledged that he had been blessed because God interceded and acted on his behalf. Jacob's heart had changed. He saw that every good thing he had was because God is who He says He is.

We should remember that, as well. When things go wrong, we eagerly blame God. But when we experience prosperity, we easily take the glory for ourselves.

Jacob Was Satisfied

Jacob lived much of his life like an orphan—so terrified God wouldn't provide that he resorted to stealing from and deceiving people, including Laban. But as he began to believe God was with him and for him, Jacob let go of those impulses.

We see this when Laban came to Jacob with accusations flying. He accused Jacob of being deceitful and stealing from him, but Jacob responded with calm assurance:

> **"Before our relatives, point out anything that is yours and take it"** (Genesis 31:32).

Jacob had overcome his desire to steal. He knew God was willing and able to give him more than he needed, and he was free to be satisfied with that provision.

Jacob Turned to God

The theme of Jacob's new hope in God continued when he prepared to encounter his brother Esau for the first time since they had parted ways all those years ago.

When Jacob heard that Esau was bringing 400 men for the reunion, Jacob became filled with fear. His old battle with anxiety rose up again, but this time he handled things better. Instead of running into his tent and making a plan to deceive Esau before Esau could deceive him, Jacob turned to God:

> **"Then Jacob said, 'God of my father Abraham and God of my father Isaac, the LORD who said to me, "Go back to your land and to your family, and I will cause you to prosper," I am unworthy of all the kindness and faithfulness You have shown Your servant. Indeed, I crossed over this Jordan with my staff, and now I have become two camps. Please rescue me from the hand of my brother Esau, for I am afraid of him; otherwise, he may come and attack me, the mothers, and their children. You have said, "I will cause you to prosper, and I will make your offspring like the sand of the sea, which cannot be counted"'"** (Genesis 32:9-12).

Watch the *Creation Restored* video "God's Love Goes Further," available at *threadsmedia.com/creationrestored.*

Jacob was still afraid. He was still anxious. But he'd changed, and he turned to God for salvation instead of trying to save himself.

Compare Genesis 12:1-3 and 32:9-12. What are the similarities and differences between the calls of Abram and Jacob?

None of these were small changes. God delivered Jacob from the sin that had entangled him throughout his entire life. But God's redemption didn't stop with Jacob's heart. God also transformed and deepened the relationship between Jacob and Himself.

JACOB'S RELATIONSHIP WITH GOD HAD CHANGED
Jacob prepared to meet Esau by moving his family and all his possessions to a place where they'd be safe, and then he was left alone to wonder what the next day might hold. You can imagine Jacob's sleepless night. He made all the plans he could, he poured out his prayers to God, and still he was left to sit and wait in a bed of anxiety, working through all the ways he could talk Esau out of destroying him.

Then things got weird:

> "Jacob was left alone, and a man wrestled with him until daybreak. When the man saw that He could not defeat him, He struck Jacob's hip socket as they wrestled and dislocated his hip. Then He said to Jacob, 'Let Me go, for it is daybreak.' But Jacob said, 'I will not let You go unless You bless me'" (Genesis 32:24-26).

Who was this guy? Why did he want to wrestle? And after the guy knocked Jacob's hip out of whack with a single blow, why didn't Jacob get away from him as fast as possible?

Jacob understood what was happening before we do. He understood he was seeing "God face to face" and was still alive, and he refused to let God go without receiving a blessing. The results were interesting:

> "'What is your name?' the man asked.

> "'Jacob,' he replied.

> "'Your name will no longer be Jacob,' He said. 'It will be Israel because you have struggled with God and with men and have prevailed'" (vv. 27-28).

God changed Jacob's name, just like He changed Abraham's. But first, God made Jacob admit who he was—Jacob literally means "he grasps the heel," which was a term for deception. Jacob was a deceiver. But then God gave Jacob a new name, Israel, because he had "struggled with God and men and prevailed."

Jacob had been wrestling his whole life, but in that moment he heard something new from the voice of God: Rest. You have prevailed.

He prevailed by learning to hang on to God. Jacob, who used to run from God, became a man who refused to let go of God. Jacob, who had walked arrogantly his whole life, earned a limp as evidence that God had blessed him with a unique, precious encounter—one that would leave him changed forever.

What have been the high points of your life so far? When have you prevailed?

We all want moments like that in our stories. We want an encounter that leaves us changed and walking differently for the rest of our lives. The problem comes with the rest of the story. After Jacob wrestled with God, he didn't become a Christian superhero. He was still a sinner. He still disobeyed God.

And so will we.

We'll have moments with God that are life-transforming, but these moments can't be the source of our hope to be changed. God didn't set our lives up so that we'd put our hope in emotional experiences or individual moments. He wants us to find our hope in Him alone.

Sanctification is confusing. We know God values change, and He wants to fully restore our relationships with Him. So we think that our desire for a single moment that will change everything honors Him—but God isn't interested in sanctification that doesn't lead to dependence. The plan He has for us isn't one-and-done; it's a moment-by-moment need for Him that will continue from now until heaven.

When have you encountered God in a transformational way?

What prevents you from putting your hope in those moments rather than in God?

Listen to "A Last Time for Everything" by Ben Shive from the *Creation Restored* playlist, available at *threadsmedia.com/creationrestored.*

JACOB'S RELATIONSHIPS WITH OTHERS HAD CHANGED

The next morning, after his amazing experience with God, Jacob went out to face his fear and meet his brother. When he saw his brother coming in the distance, he prepared for the worst. He laid himself on the ground, ready to receive the just punishment for the times he'd betrayed and deceived his brother.

> **"But Esau ran to meet him, hugged him, threw his arms around him, and kissed him. Then they wept" (Genesis 33:4).**

After all the stress, anxiety, and strategies for how to protect his family and possessions, Jacob finally saw what was in Esau's mind and heart—but it wasn't the hatred and destruction Jacob anticipated. Instead, he found himself face-to-face with his own wasted worry in the tears of Esau.

Too many of us live our lives in a constant state of preparation for the events of tomorrow. In this story, however, God proved to Jacob that His grace is sufficient for today. No amount of planning could have prepared Jacob for the sweetness of this reunion.

Jacob had been waiting for Esau's approval his whole life, and then—in a single moment— he had it. But the night that had preceded that moment and the days and the years that had come before had made a different man out of Jacob.

> **"But Jacob said, 'No, please! If I have found favor with you, take this gift from my hand. For indeed, I have seen your face, and it is like seeing God's face, since you have accepted me. Please take my present that was brought to you, because God has been gracious to me and I have everything I need.' So Jacob urged him until he accepted" (Genesis 33:10-11).**

Jacob wanted to bless Esau, but not in order to earn his brother's acceptance. He wanted to bless Esau because God had been gracious to him, and he had everything he needed.

That should be one of our life verses. It's the key to our peace. It's the key to restoring relationships and "happily ever afters." If we believe God is dealing graciously with us and if we believe we have everything we need in Him, we'll be freed up to bless others like Jacob was.

Life can seem like a big, fat mess. Maybe you can relate to that. But here in the pages of Genesis we find a tiny, treasured truth: The solution to our anxiety and fear isn't more planning and strategizing about how to change our circumstances. Rather, it's deep faith that God is dealing graciously with us and an understanding that we have enough.

 "Therefore don't worry about tomorrow, because tomorrow will worry about itself. Each day has enough trouble of its own" (Matthew 6:34).

HAPPILY EVER AFTER?

We've arrived at the "happily ever after" moment—a great place to wrap up the story. Jacob had been saved by God. He was redeemed. His relationships were restored.

In that moment, Jacob could have stood in front of a room of believers and shared a testimony that would leave them in tears. A broken, desperate man, estranged from his family, entangled by sin, and running from God; he had been a deceitful sinner pursued by a loving Father until he was freed from sin, and all the people he had wronged greeted him with tenderness.

That's the gospel. It's the story of how love changes a person. We've seen that theme over and over again throughout the stories of Genesis.

If Jacob's life were a movie or a fairy tale, it would end here. But God refused to end Jacob's story that way. He won't let us think His love is the same as our limited human version. God's love is strong enough to change us, yes. It's strong enough to pull us out of the pit. It's strong enough to redeem and restore. But His love goes further still.

God's love is strong enough to endure, even when we wander once again. His love endures even if we gaze at the strength of His love and experience an amazing encounter with Him—then walk out the door and forget everything and fail Him all over again. God doesn't grow weary of displaying faithfulness to us.

No matter how badly we want sin to be part of our past, it's not. It's part of our present. No matter how many times we have nights like Jacob's, we still find the rebellion in our hearts seeking to entangle us in the morning light.

God loves us beyond those moments and into the next chapter. He loves us enough to save us every moment of every day for the rest of our lives.

His love goes further still.

Are there any Bible characters who had a true "happily ever after" ending to their stories? If so, who?

How do you react to the idea that God's love "goes further" than all of your rebellion and sin?

THE REST OF THE STORY

What happened next is more than a little discouraging. At the end of Genesis 33, we learn that Jacob—the same guy who had just seen God face to face and been reunited with his brother—responded by failing to obey God. Instead of "and they all lived happily ever after," we get, "and Jacob continued to sin."

> "After Jacob came from Paddan-aram, he arrived safely at Shechem in the land of Canaan and camped in front of the city. He purchased a section of the field where he had pitched his tent from the sons of Hamor, Shechem's father, for 100 qesitahs. And he set up an altar there and called it 'God, the God of Israel'" (Genesis 33:18-19).

Jacob was on his way to his homeland, just like God commanded. But when he arrived in the city of Shechem, he decided to ignore God's call and instead bought some land and settled down. He even set up an altar in that town, naming it "God, the God of Israel." In other words, he made a commitment to worship God even as he disobeyed God.

We can relate to this. We raise our hands in worship on Sunday even as our hearts plot ways to avoid God's call on our lives. We justify decisions we know are wrong with the promise that we'll make it up to God through worship. We have amazing encounters with God then walk out the door and run straight into the arms of sin.

No matter how emotional or special, a single encounter with God doesn't hold the key to transformation. Sin is still crouching at the door, and it knows we have short memories. Sooner or later, we will fall again.

What other people in the Bible failed after a profound encounter with God?

Jacob decided to move into a city and mix with people who worshiped false gods. That decision led to a pretty dark turn:

> "Dinah, Leah's daughter whom she bore to Jacob, went out to see some of the young women of the area. When Shechem son of Hamor the Hivite, a prince of the region, saw her, he took her and raped her. He became infatuated with Dinah, daughter of Jacob. He loved the young girl and spoke tenderly to her. 'Get me this girl as a wife,' he told his father Hamor" (Genesis 34:1-4).

 Leading a group? It's the way to go. Find extra questions and teaching tools in the leader kit, available at *threadsmedia.com/creationrestored.*

After learning what had happened, Dinah's brothers became filled with rage. As the sons of Jacob the deceiver, they initiated a deception of their own in order to take justice into their own hands. They declared that Shechem could only marry Dinah if every male in the city was circumcised. Then, when all the men were too weak to fight, the brothers killed them all and took the women of the city for their own.

Think about that: The brothers took circumcision, a sign of God's great love and faithfulness to His covenant people, and used it as a tool to deceive, murder, and destroy.

Jacob's response was almost as discouraging:

> **"Then Jacob said to Simeon and Levi, 'You have brought trouble on me, making me odious to the inhabitants of the land, the Canaanites and the Perizzites. We are few in number; if they unite against me and attack me, I and my household will be destroyed'" (Genesis 34:30).**

Jacob's daughter had been raped and his sons had committed murder, but his main concern was that he might lose his possessions. He totally ignored the morality of the situation. He responded with the same fear and anxiety that had characterized most of his life.

This is devastating. If we had stopped the story just a little bit earlier, we could have believed that Jacob was truly delivered from his life long battle with fear. Instead, we read about him sitting there, once again obsessed and motivated by self-preservation, unable to trust God.

GOD'S RESPONSE

After reading all that, we can't help but brace ourselves for the worst. What punishment will God send to Jacob and his sons? How will God discipline people whose hearts were so crooked?

We've all forgiven people we thought had changed, only to be hurt again by them. We've all put faith in people who appeared to be transformed, only to watch them fall back into old patterns. So part of us wants Jacob to get what's coming to him.

On the flip side, we've all been Jacob. We've been rescued from our battle with jealousy only to feel it creep back into our hearts. Or we've been freed from addictions, and then one day we're forced to wrestle with our failures again. Or we've defeated anger problems, only to see them come crashing back when we least expect it.

God responded in three ways, and they were all shocking in light of the situation.

1. God Spoke to Jacob

Look at Genesis 35:1:

> "God said to Jacob, 'Get up! Go to Bethel and settle there. Build an altar there to the God who appeared to you when you fled from your brother Esau.'"

God responded to Jacob's anxiety by reminding him of the initial call and command that led him away from Laban. God didn't say, "I told you so!" He didn't point out that Jacob's disobedience triggered this tragic chain of events. Instead, God renewed His call on Jacob's life.

And Jacob obeyed—again:

> "So Jacob said to his family and all who were with him, 'Get rid of the foreign gods that are among you. Purify yourselves and change your clothes. We must get up and go to Bethel. I will build an altar there to the God who answered me in my day of distress. He has been with me everywhere I have gone'" (Genesis 35:2-3).

Take note of the order here. God didn't affirm His love and call on Jacob's life after Jacob repented. It was God's reminder of His faithfulness that led Jacob to repent. God's faithfulness doesn't wait for an apology. His faithfulness leads us to that apology.

Still, we wonder why God didn't at least yell at Jacob first. Why didn't He make Jacob suffer a little before affirming His promises? Because no matter how deep you think love can go, God's love goes further still.

What were the short-term and long-term consequences of Jacob's disobedience?

Does it rub you the wrong way that Jacob wasn't punished? Why or why not?

2. God Protected Jacob

Jacob didn't pause to worry before obeying God this time. His greatest fear—that the other nations would attack him because of what his sons had done—was directly in front of him. He had to walk through their lands in order to get to Bethel, but he didn't hesitate.

 Jacob gave the name Bethel to the place where God first spoke to him through a dream (see Genesis 28:10-22). Bethel means "house of God."

Verse 5 explains why:

> **"When they set out, a terror from God came over the cities around them, and they did not pursue Jacob's sons."**

Here's the catch: Jacob and his sons deserved to be attacked. They deserved to be destroyed by those other cities. Yet God intervened and protected them. This wasn't God protecting the righteous from unjust persecution; this was God protecting the unrighteous from just persecution. God was protecting Jacob from what he deserved.

This kind of love makes no sense to us. While we cross our arms and demand consequences for sinners, God intervenes and protects those of us who are His, even when we don't deserve protection.

Is God unjust? Is He unwilling to punish sin? Why didn't He at least remove His hand enough to teach Jacob that he couldn't always count on protection when he stepped outside God's will? Because no matter how much we think we understand God's grace, His love goes further still.

3. God Blessed Jacob

Look at what happened after Jacob arrived:

> **"God appeared to Jacob again after he returned from Paddan-aram, and He blessed him. God said to him: 'Your name is Jacob; you will no longer be named Jacob, but your name will be Israel.'**
>
> **"So He named him Israel. God also said to him: 'I am God Almighty. Be fruitful and multiply. A nation, indeed an assembly of nations, will come from you, and kings will descend from you. I will give to you the land that I gave to Abraham and Isaac. And I will give the land to your future descendants'"** (Genesis 35:9-12).

God wasn't done with Jacob. He didn't remind Jacob that they'd had this exact conversation before. Instead, God spoke the blessing and the covenant to Jacob as if it were the first time. It's like *Groundhog Day* (the movie, not the actual day).

Why didn't God remove Jacob from his chosen position or at least bench him for a little while? Was he honestly still fit to be the father of God's people? Didn't God grow weary of reminding Jacob of His faithfulness? You know the answer to those questions by now.

No matter how much God's love moves our hearts, makes us cry, and overwhelms us when we see how far it stretches and how much it endures, know this: His love goes further still.

What does our culture communicate about the "proper" boundaries and limits of love?

What does the church communicate about those boundaries and limits?

THE GOSPEL AND GOD'S FAITHFULNESS

We're all recovering from failure, walking in failure, or about to walk in failure. The great news is that wherever you fall on that line, the gospel is for you.

Wherever you are in the midst of your failure, God speaks to you and protects you and blesses you (if you are in Christ).

So hear Him speak. Hear His kindness now. God isn't angry with you. He is speaking to you in the midst of your failure, reminding you of His faithfulness in the past, and reminding you of His call on your life. He's calling you back to obedience and back to worship. Let that call empower you to turn from your sin and walk toward Him without fear or anxiety over what it will cost you.

Let Him protect you. Walk faithfully to what God has called you to do, knowing that He's shielding you in Christ from what you deserve because of your sin. God is just, but the consequences you deserve have been paid in full on the cross. Even now, Jesus lives to intercede for you. Even now, His blood is precious enough to pay for your sins—not just yesterday's failures, but today's. And tomorrow's.

Let Him bless you. God crushed His own Son because He wanted to bless you. He will graciously give you all things, not because you've earned them, but because Christ earned them on your behalf.

When Jacob first encountered God in a dream all those years ago, we saw the gospel. We saw that God was willing to come down from heaven and make a way for Jacob to know Him. The gospel was and is the only way to have a relationship with God.

When Jacob continued to grow and work through all the brokenness in his life, we saw the gospel. We saw that God was willing not just to save His children, but to refine and change them over time. The gospel was and is the only way to be changed.

But the gospel isn't just made for the beginning of the story. The gospel isn't just made to sweep in through one powerful, transforming encounter. The gospel is made for each moment of every day.

Gospel testimonies don't have an ending; they don't have a "happily ever after" this side of heaven. Our stories get to proclaim that God's love is greater than any love we've ever known. Our stories go on and on because the gospel is constantly saving and constantly changing us.

And when you think you've reached the end of His love, it goes further still. Trust me. When you see how deep your sin really runs, His love goes further still. When you think you've betrayed Him one too many times, His love goes further still.

Always.

APPLY TO LIFE

Start a discussion with a friend or spouse this week by asking about the other person's favorite "happily ever after" ending to a story or movie. (Be prepared to talk about your favorite ending, as well.) Then ask: "What would a 'happily ever after' ending look like for your life?"

Using the space on pages 90–91, write down any prolonged conflicts you have been involved in during your life—times when you held a grudge against another person, or timed when others held a grudge against you. Under each of these conflicts, answer the following questions:

1. What started the conflict?
2. What is the current status of the conflict?
3. What's one thing you could do to improve your relationship with the person in question?

Take a moment to think of two or more people who are considered "failures" in your community. Commit to making contact with at least one of these individuals this week in order to be a blessing.

THE GOD WHO SPEAKS IN SILENCE

GENESIS 37–42

SESSION FIVE

"Long ago God spoke to the fathers by the prophets at different times and in different ways. In these last days, He has spoken to us by His Son. God has appointed Him heir of all things and made the universe through Him" (Hebrews 1:1-2).

ave you ever been in a situation so bleak that you cried out: Where is God in all this? Why is He silent?" I (Halim) have. I know what it feels like to be tossed around by life.

We all have moments like that—times when we find ourselves in the dark and we feel more alone and forsaken than we imagined possible. Every Christian will have to face questions like: Where is God when it all falls apart? And why does He seem so silent?

The way you answer those questions will determine the trajectory of your life. That's because the way you answer those questions will determine if suffering drives you toward God or away from Him.

Some people conclude that God is dead. Perhaps the seeming silence from heaven sounds so deafening because there's no one up there to speak. Perhaps God is no more than a fantasy in our heads, and the absence of His tangible, audible presence in suffering reveals that.

Others conclude God is cruel. After all, if we had the power to reach out and touch those who are hurting—to somehow make them feel less alone, or even to heal them—we would. So how could God be kind and still seem so distant?

Still others conclude that God is hands-off. They know He's real, and they know all this pain exists, so the only way to make sense of the world is to limit His power. It must be that He has chosen, in His great wisdom, to give up His rule over the earth. He's set up the universe like some cosmic wind-up toy, and now He's watching it all unfold just like the rest of us. He's wondering how it will turn out, but He's powerless to fix it, just like the rest of us.

Those are terrifying conclusions. If we believe any one of those ideas, we'll become hopeless in our suffering. If God is dead, our lives are meaningless. If God is cruel, where can we go for safety? If God is hands-off, then we're like ping-pong balls bouncing between Satan, sin, and fate.

What options would you add to the ones mentioned above?

Those of us attempting to follow Jesus don't believe God is dead. We don't believe He's cruel, and we don't believe He's weak or that He's not the ruler of this world. That's the good news.

Listen to "Bend (Joseph)" by Brandon Heath from the *Creation Restored* playlist, available at *threadsmedia.com/creationrestored*.

SESSION FIVE CREATION RESTORED

The bad news is that we often choose Option D: None of the above. We avoid the question altogether. When those moments of pain and suffering come and God seems to be silent, we tell our friends (and ourselves) that God is just "mysterious." We say: "No one can know why this suffering is happening or why God seems so silent. God is a mystery. We can't know what He's thinking."

The only problem with that theory is the Bible. If we want to live our lives under the "mystery" worldview, we'll have to avoid the Book of Genesis, among other things.

There are thousands of things we aren't told about God—that's true. But there are also thousands of things we are told about Him. We can't always understand God's purposes, and we'll never fully grasp His hidden will, but we can certainly bank on the truth of what He tells us.

That's the great thing about the Bible. Through God's Word, we can answer questions about who He is and why He does the things He does. Through the stories in the pages of Genesis, we can see what God is really up to when He seems silent in our suffering.

INTRODUCING JOSEPH
So far in this study we've seen good times with Abraham and a bit of a bumpier road with Jacob. As we move on to Genesis 37, the focus shifts to Joseph, who at the time was Jacob's youngest son.

The first 11 verses of that chapter catch us up on what we need to know:

- **He was 17 years old.**
- **He was a tattle-tale.** Joseph's first recorded action in the Bible was bringing a "bad report" of his brothers to his father.
- **He was his daddy's favorite.** Jacob "loved Joseph more than his other sons"—so much so that he made Joseph a robe of many colors. For us, that just sounds like a great idea for a musical, but the original hearers would have known that Jacob was bestowing upon Joseph the privileges usually given to a firstborn son.
- **He was not his brothers' favorite.** His brothers saw their father's elevation of Joseph and hated him for it.

We know from the text that Joseph was a prophet appointed to rise above his brothers. He was given a dream from God where he and his brothers were all binding sheaves of grain in the field. All of a sudden, Joseph's sheaf stood up, and the sheaves of his brothers gathered around and bowed down to it.

 The end of Genesis 35 informs us that both Rachel (vv. 16-20) and Isaac (vv. 27-29) died before Joseph turned 17.

Joseph had a second dream where his whole family was represented by stars (his siblings) and the sun and moon (his parents). Again, they all bowed down to him.

We can also infer from the text that Joseph was arrogant. For one thing, he told his family about his dreams and everyone bowing down to him and all that—twice. And when he told them, he used an exalted, commanding tone. Looking at Joseph's words in the original language, it's as if he was saying: "Stand in awe! I'm going to rule over you! Look! I will be bowed down to by you!"

As we've already discussed, the older sons were supposed to rule over the younger siblings in that culture. So it was extremely controversial and offensive for the youngest to talk about ruling over the oldest—not to mention the parents!

As readers, this window into Joseph's life and attitude prepares us for what happened next.

JOSEPH'S TERRIBLE, HORRIBLE, NO GOOD, VERY BAD DAY

One day, Jacob sent Joseph to the fields to track down his brothers while they were herding sheep. But he couldn't find them in their usual spot. *Coincidentally*, he ran into a man out there in the middle of nowhere, and the man approached Joseph and asked what he was looking for. *Coincidentally*, the man had seen the brothers earlier, and the man happened to overhear where the brothers were heading.

The only place we usually find this number of coincidences is in a romantic comedy, but (unfortunately for Joseph) this wasn't that kind of story. Circumstances seemed to be conspiring against Joseph to produce a really bad day. Here's what happened next:

> **"They saw him in the distance, and before he had reached them, they plotted to kill him. They said to one another, 'Here comes that dreamer! Come on, let's kill him and throw him into one of the pits. We can say that a vicious animal ate him. Then we'll see what becomes of his dreams!'" (Genesis 37:18-20).**

What disagreements or circumstances have caused conflict in your family?

Reuben, the oldest brother, was the voice of grace in the situation. He suggested that instead of physically harming Joseph, they just leave him in a pit to die. Reuben planned to go back and rescue Joseph later, so his heart was in the right place. But he didn't have the courage to fully stand up to his younger brothers.

 Joseph travelled about 50 miles to reach Shechem, and then another 15 miles to reach his brothers in Dothan.

SESSION FIVE CREATION RESTORED

"When Joseph came to his brothers, they stripped off his robe, the robe of many colors that he had on. Then they took him and threw him into the pit. The pit was empty; there was no water in it. Then they sat down to eat a meal" (vv. 23-25).

They sat down to eat a meal!? Try to wrap your head around the level of brokenness that must have existed in that family. These guys threw their own brother in a pit to die, and instead of showing any remorse or guilt, they sat down to eat. They were totally at ease with their actions.

Coincidentally, a caravan of Ishmaelites came down the road as they were eating. And that's when Judah started seeing dollar signs. He pointed out that "just" killing Joseph wouldn't really benefit anyone. Wouldn't it make more sense to sell him as a slave? That way they could get rid of him, they wouldn't have his blood on their hands, and they could make some cash. After all, Judah concluded, "he is our brother, our own flesh."

Meanwhile, Reuben had gone off to rescue Joseph, but the timing didn't work out and he missed his window. By the time he reached the pit, Joseph was gone.

That's how Joseph was removed from his family. A thousand details, a thousand chance encounters, a thousand cases of bad timing, and they all added up to a teenager, beaten and bruised, rolling down the road with nothing but a life of slavery in front of him.

You have to wonder if Joseph replayed all the details of the day as he sat in that caravan on his way to Egypt. If only his father hadn't sent him out to his brothers. If only the man hadn't seen him and told him where his brothers were. If only the man hadn't overheard correctly. If only Reuben had gotten there in time. *If only.*

Sometimes God seems silent in our suffering because we can't hear Him over the nagging doubts in our hearts. Sometimes we're so busy playing out scenarios of how things might have been different that we don't have ears to hear God speaking in the middle of our suffering. *If only I was thinner. If only I was smarter. If only I was richer. If only that light had been green. If only I had known.*

What are some "if only" moments you've been thinking about in recent months?

What situations or activities help you hear God most clearly?

 Verse 28 says that Joseph was sold for "20 pieces of silver," which was the standard fee for a teenage slave (see Leviticus 27:5).

Unless we silence those "if only" moments, we'll have a hard time hearing the gentle, loving whisper of God working behind the scenes in our circumstances to bring us good through our suffering.

Once Joseph was gone, the "band of brothers" still had a mess to clean up. Here's what they did:

> "So they took Joseph's robe, slaughtered a young goat, and dipped the robe in its blood. They sent the robe of many colors to their father and said, 'We found this. Examine it. Is it your son's robe or not?'
>
> His father recognized it. 'It is my son's robe,' he said. 'A vicious animal has devoured him. Joseph has been torn to pieces!' Then Jacob tore his clothes, put sackcloth around his waist, and mourned for his son many days. All his sons and daughters tried to comfort him, but he refused to be comforted. 'No,' he said. 'I will go down to Sheol to my son, mourning.' And his father wept for him" (vv. 31-35).

Again, how dysfunctional was this family? When the brothers held out the robe to Jacob, they couldn't even use Joseph's name. They merely referred to him as "your son," as if they didn't know him.

Then, when Jacob became lost in a cloud of grief, the brothers gathered around him with the rest of the family and "tried to comfort him." Tried! They could see their actions were destroying their father, and they knew how to make things right—yet they refused. They stayed silent. Think about how deep their hatred and brokenness must have run.

Of course, Joseph's brothers weren't the only ones who stayed quiet. God's name isn't mentioned throughout the entire chapter, nor was His voice heard.

God was silent, too.

Look at Genesis 4:1-16. What are the similarities and differences between Cain's actions and the actions of Joseph's brothers?

What are the similarities and differences between God's responses in both situations?

 Watch the *Creation Restored* video "The God Who Speaks in Silence," available at *threadsmedia.com/creationrestored*.

It's hard to imagine what Joseph must have gone through during those early months in Egypt; it's even harder to imagine his heart toward God. Was he bitter? Did he feel mocked by the memory of the dreams God had given to him? Did he have any hope at all?

My guess is that he wrestled through a lot of questions: *Has sin ruined my life? Am I a slave to circumstance? Where is God in all of this? Why doesn't He speak?*

We still ask those questions today when it seems like the world is conspiring against us and God is nowhere to be found.

Where is God when a tiny miscommunication creates a huge problem at work, and what was supposed to be a promotion becomes a pink slip? Where is God when you hear about another teenager committing suicide because of bullying that was triggered by the absence of parents in another child's life? Where is God when you get the call that one person running late for work caused a wreck that cost you your family?

Maybe you're asking those kinds of questions right now. Maybe you know what it's like to wake up and look around the shambles of your life and wonder where everything went wrong. You lift your hands to heaven, desperate to hear from God—but there's no audible voice, no writing on the wall.

It all boils down to two questions: If God is in control, why doesn't He fix our lives? If God is so good, why doesn't He show up in a way we can see, hear, and touch?

Let's stay with Joseph and find out.

GOD WAS IN CONTROL

Joseph knew God. He was the son of Jacob—a descendent of Isaac and Abraham. He'd heard the stories about those great men.

God had spoken directly to Abraham, calling him to a new land and establishing a covenant with his family. God had directly intervened in the pairing of Isaac and Rebekah. And God had wrestled with Jacob—physically touching him so that every limping step he took reminded him of God's reality and presence.

That being the case, when Joseph was dragged out of his familiar life and thrown into something new and terrible, he must have been very aware that the same things weren't happening to him. And we know from the text that Joseph's life went from bad to worse over the next 13 years.

 "LORD, I call to You; my rock, do not be deaf to me. If You remain silent to me, I will be like those going down to the Pit" (Psalm 28:1).

We also know that, no matter how bad things felt to Joseph, God was in control. With the Bible in our hands, we can say for sure that every act of failure and misguided circumstance was an instrument in the hands of a mighty, loving God.

The same is true for us. God is fully in control of our lives. He rules over all things. Even in the moments when He seems silent and distant, we can trust in the truth that He is sovereignly, lovingly steering our lives in their perfect directions to fulfill His purpose.

We know that because of the rest of Joseph's story and because of the rest of the Bible.

THE REST OF JOSEPH'S STORY

The next years of Joseph's life became a cycle of suffering. Each time things began to look up, the bottom was pulled out once again, and Joseph would find himself in a new kind of affliction.

But there was a second theme underlying Joseph's story during those years. We see it when he first began working as a slave for Potiphar:

> "Now Joseph had been taken to Egypt. An Egyptian named Potiphar, an officer of Pharaoh and the captain of the guard, bought him from the Ishmaelites who had brought him there. The LORD was with Joseph, and he became a successful man, serving in the household of his Egyptian master. When his master saw that the LORD was with him and that the LORD made everything he did successful, Joseph found favor in his master's sight and became his personal attendant. Potiphar also put him in charge of his household and placed all that he owned under his authority" (Genesis 39:1-4).

We see it again after Joseph was thrown in prison for a crime he didn't commit:

> "But the LORD was with Joseph and extended kindness to him. He granted him favor in the eyes of the prison warden. The warden put all the prisoners who were in the prison under Joseph's authority, and he was responsible for everything that was done there. The warden did not bother with anything under Joseph's authority, because the LORD was with him, and the LORD made everything that he did successful" (Genesis 39:21-23).

Through all the ups and downs, the coming of hope followed by renewed suffering, "the LORD was with Joseph."

 Listen to "Heaven Fall Down" by Phil Wickham from the *Creation Restored* playlist, available at *threadsmedia.com/creationrestored.*

SESSION FIVE CREATION RESTORED

Of course, it's helpful for us to see that God was with Joseph during those years of trial—it helps us feel better about what happened. But Joseph didn't get to read his life in retrospect. He didn't see the words written in the text. When Joseph looked at the details of his life as they were happening, it must have seemed like God was missing; it must have seemed like God had forsaken him or was unable to help.

So why doesn't the text record any outbursts from Joseph toward God? Why don't we read about him raising his fist in anger? Why don't we read about him demanding that God explain Himself?

The answer is that Joseph didn't walk by sight; he walked by faith. He believed in the sovereignty and kindness of God. He believed that God controlled the situation and was on his side.

Joseph's perception of reality didn't shape his beliefs. His beliefs shaped his perception of reality. He saw all the details of sin and circumstance as building blocks for the life God was building for him. Joseph trusted that God was ordaining all the coincidences and trials that came his way. And he was right.

Here's something worth remembering: Satan and fate may appear to conspire against us at times, but they are also tools for God's work.

I know that makes some people cringe. Many of us are embarrassed by the idea that God is in control of suffering. The last thing we want to tell our friend whose family member just died in a car accident is that God ordained such a tremendous tragedy. We would rather cover for God by making Him seem sweet, but uninvolved.

After all, how can God be kind if He allowed the cancer eating away at our mothers' bodies? How can God be kind if He allowed the singleness making us feel a new kind of lonely? How can God be kind if He allowed that broken relationship, that dysfunctional marriage, that sexual abuse?

What is your answer to those questions?

If we're to understand God's sovereignty, we must hold fast to God's goodness. If we're to understand God's kindness, we must also hold fast to His sovereignty. We can't diminish one truth about Him in order to elevate another.

We can't try to hold on to our "kind" God by saying He wasn't in control of the situation, thus sacrificing His sovereignty. And we can't try to hold on to our "sovereign" God by saying that He's just an angry God who punishes sin wherever He finds it.

The God that the Bible reveals to us is both sovereign and good.

THE REST OF THE BIBLE

God wants us to grasp that He's fully in control of our suffering. It's something He talks about often throughout His Word, including these passages:

> "I form light and create darkness, I make success and create disaster; I, Yahweh, do all these things" (Isaiah 45:7).

> "For His dominion is an everlasting dominion, and His kingdom is from generation to generation. All the inhabitants of the earth are counted as nothing, and He does what He wants with the army of heaven and the inhabitants of the earth. There is no one who can hold back His hand or say to Him, 'What have you done?'" (Daniel 4:34-35).

God rules over chance:

> "The lot is cast into the lap, but its every decision is from the LORD" (Proverbs 16:33).

God rules over sin and suffering:

> "Who is there who speaks and it happens, unless the Lord has ordained it? Do not both adversity and good come from the mouth of the Most High?" (Lamentations 3:37-38).

The declarations of Scripture are clear: God rules our lives. He is in control.

What situations in your life feel out of control right now?

Does it help or hurt to think that God ordained those situations and is fully in control of what's happening?

GOD WAS KIND

Not only was God in control of Joseph's situation, He demonstrated kindness by ordaining Joseph's suffering.

It's true! God's actions in Joseph's life provided solutions for two problems—one temporary and the other permanent. We'll start with the temporary problem.

Mouths to Feed

After many years in prison, Joseph was called before Pharaoh to interpret two of the Egyptian leader's dreams. What he said sent shockwaves through the room:

> "It is just as I told Pharaoh: God has shown Pharaoh what He is about to do. Seven years of great abundance are coming throughout the land of Egypt. After them, seven years of famine will take place, and all the abundance in the land of Egypt will be forgotten. The famine will devastate the land. The abundance in the land will not be remembered because of the famine that follows it, for the famine will be very severe" (Genesis 41:28-31).

In an agrarian world, seven years of famine was a big deal. It was seriously bad news. But through Joseph's 13 years of suffering, God had provided a solution.

Specifically, Joseph became second in command throughout all of Egypt—he had more power than everyone but Pharaoh. And Joseph used that power to set up a food bank that stored food during the seven years of abundance, then re-distributed it during the seven years of famine.

As a side note, remember the promises God had made to Abraham decades earlier? One of them went like this:

> "I will indeed bless you and make your offspring as numerous as the stars of the sky and the sand on the seashore. Your offspring will possess the gates of their enemies. And all the nations of the earth will be blessed by your offspring because you have obeyed My command" (Genesis 22:17-18).

God used Joseph to keep that promise. Because of his suffering, Joseph was in a position to provide food to starving people not just in Egypt, but from all over the world:

> "Every nation came to Joseph in Egypt to buy grain, for the famine was severe in every land" (Genesis 41:57).

 Leading a group? It's the way to go. Find extra questions and teaching tools in the leader kit, available at *threadsmedia.com/creationrestored*.

In other words, "all of the nations of the earth" were blessed through Joseph. He may have been the first man in his family who didn't have an audible "conversation" with God, but he was also the first man in his family given the opportunity to be a tangible part of bringing God's promises to fruition.

Souls to Save

Through God's kindness, Joseph was able to save several thousand people from starvation and death—including his own family back in the land of Canaan:

> **"When Jacob learned that there was grain in Egypt, he said to his sons, 'Why do you keep looking at each other? Listen,' he went on, 'I have heard there is grain in Egypt. Go down there and buy some for us so that we will live and not die'" (Genesis 42:1-2).**

That was a temporary matter, but God also used Joseph's suffering to pave the way for a permanent solution to the problem of sin and death.

God's promise that "all the nations of the earth" would be blessed by Abraham's offspring was partially fulfilled through Joseph, but of course we know the ultimate blessing of Abraham's line was the promised Messiah, Jesus Christ. If Jacob and his children had perished in that famine, however, God's promise would never have come true.

Sometimes we read about Joseph's suffering and think, *How could God let that happen to someone He loved?* But if we keep the whole story in mind, we'll think: *Aha! That's how God's people arrived in Egypt! That's how God provided a way for His people to survive the devastating famine that was just a few years down the road.*

What's more, we'll think: *That's how God preserved the family of His promise and maintained His plan for our salvation through Jesus Christ.*

Don't let that truth slip away unnoticed. In His kindness, God ordained that Joseph should suffer for 13 long years. And if the chain of events hadn't gone exactly that way, Joseph would have died. His brothers would have died. The entire nation of Israel would have been cut off before ever having a chance to flower, and God's promises would have been forfeit.

The same is true for us. Whatever we're struggling through right now, unless the details of that suffering happened exactly the way they happened, we'd be in serious trouble. Even with the sin and circumstances involved, even with each missed opportunity and each example of tragic timing—things happened the way they happened because God is kind and He's in control.

GOD WAS SPEAKING

One other element of Joseph's story needs to be explored: God's apparent silence in the midst of Joseph's suffering. This is the element that can feel the most frustrating when we experience it today.

We can see the ways suffering has shaped us and brought us to where we are. We understand that God is sovereign, and we can even get on board with the idea that our suffering demonstrates His kindness.

What is harder to understand is why the experience of suffering has to feel so incredibly isolating—why God seems so silent. We are willing to walk through the pain, if necessary; we just want some kind of assurance that God is with us. We want a word from Him.

At what point in your past did you feel most isolated from God?

What helped you get through that situation and find a deeper connection with Him?

In reality, sometimes what seems like silence to us is simply the sound of our own unbelief. Sometimes God seems silent because regardless of what we believe at the intellectual level, in our hearts we believe the lie that suffering has come our way because God isn't on our side or because He isn't in control.

Believing that God is both kind and in control frees us to hear His voice. It frees us to understand that God doesn't speak to us *during* our suffering as much as He speaks to us *through* our suffering.

God Speaks Through Suffering

Did you ever get lost as a child? At first, it's not scary at all. You wander away from your mom or dad because you see something that's shiny or interesting on the next aisle. You find yourself gazing at one distracting trinket after another. There is so much noise, so much to see, so much commotion that you have no idea you're lost. You don't feel scared or panicked because you're quite happily diverted.

But even though you don't realize it—even though your view of the world in that moment is happy and safe—you're actually in big trouble. You're in a terrifying and tremendously vulnerable position.

When the distractions are taken away for a moment or something interrupts your focus, you suddenly realize what's really going on. You reach for a parent, but no one is there. Your eyes scan the faces around you without recognizing anyone. Panic sets in. You're lost, and you know it.

You experience suffering, which makes all the distractions and noise fade away. And in that moment of clarity you hear the voice of your parent calling out for you across the store.

The same is true when we're lost today—especially when we're wandering away from our Heavenly Father.

When we go out on a perfect 70-degree day and our jobs are going great and our lives are all we'd hoped they would be, it's hard to feel like there's anything wrong with this world. When things are going great, it's hard to believe this earth isn't our home. It's hard to believe a war is going on all around us—even in our own souls. It's hard to believe we're desperately lost apart from God.

In those moments, God sometimes speaks to us by allowing us to suffer. It's His way of stopping all the diversions and distractions that keep us from seeing what's real.

When we experience suffering, we realize we're lost. We see that the things of this world are temporal and fleeting, and it scares us. Remember: Suffering is not the source of that fear. Suffering just points out what was already true.

In other words, suffering isn't the bad guy. Suffering is God's gracious provision to help us hear His voice and come running back to His side. Suffering isn't a mute button that makes it harder to hear God; it's His megaphone to speak in our lives.

Do you agree with these statements? Why or why not?

Does believing that God speaks to us through suffering make that suffering easier or harder to handle? Why?

That's what Joseph came to understand. Joseph's story doesn't include any audible or physical interactions with God. Genesis contains no record of God visiting Joseph in the night or sending him a sign as He'd done with Joseph's forefathers.

 "Pain insists upon being attended to. God whispers to us in our pleasures, speaks in our consciences, but shouts in our pain: it is His megaphone to rouse a deaf world." —C. S. Lewis[1]

SESSION FIVE CREATION RESTORED

And yet, it's clear from Joseph's life that he must have felt assured that God was for him. Even when God seemed silent, Joseph's actions prove that he knew God was speaking.

That's because Joseph had something more encouraging than a visit at night or a hug in prison from God. Joseph had a promise from God, and all the suffering in the world couldn't keep that promise quiet. The promise proclaimed God's love and encouragement to Joseph at every turn. The promise was the voice of God in those silent seasons.

Instead of letting his perception of God's silence convince Joseph that God was far way, he let the truth of God's promise shape his perception of God's silence. He was able to hear from God without any kind of audible voice because he stood on the spoken word of God that had been given all those years before. *God had already spoken.*

The same is true for us. God has spoken. He has given us His Word so that in all circumstances we can know He is with us and for us. He has given us promises written down and recorded so that we can literally wrap our arms around them and hang onto them when trials come.

When have you been most encouraged by God's Word?

Best of all, God gave us His Son.

God Has Spoken Through His Son

We often tell ourselves that if we knew for sure God was on our side—if we just knew for sure that He was still with us and hadn't left us—we'd be OK. If God interacted with us like He interacted with the prophets of old, then we wouldn't experience any doubt in the face of suffering.

But God *has* spoken to us. He proved that He is for us and that He'll never leave us, and He promised to be with us in all things. More, He sealed that promise with the blood of His Son. That's the good news of the gospel:

> **"Long ago God spoke to the fathers by the prophets at different times and in different ways. In these last days, He has spoken to us by His Son. God has appointed Him heir of all things and made the universe through Him"** (Hebrews 1:1-2).

Because of the cross, we have assurance that God is speaking to us—even when He seems silent.

 "In the beginning was the Word, and the Word was with God, and the Word was God. He was with God in the beginning" (John 1:1-2).

If ever there was a time God seemed out of control, it was the cross. If ever there was a time God looked cruel, it was the cross. And yet at no other time in history has God so magnificently displayed His sovereignty and kindness as He did through the broken body of Jesus hanging on a tree and paying for the sins of the world.

When Christ became sin and felt God's wrath poured out on Him, for the first time in eternity God's Son experienced what we so desperately fear: God was silent. As Christ became our sin, He lost the comfort of His Heavenly Father's words—the Voice Jesus had heard from before the beginning of time. As Christ became sin, God forsook Him, and Jesus' assurance that God was with Him was obliterated by the crashing descent of deafening silence.

Christ experienced the silence of God so that you and I would never have to. Christ experienced the silence of God so that we could look around at the people experiencing pain and sorrow and tell them that God is never silent with those who are in Christ.

So, when you feel the weight of God's seeming silence, look at the cross and take heart. Your God will never leave you or forsake you. You will never face His silence because Jesus faced it on your behalf.

When the crushing waves of suffering wash over your life, cling to the voice of God that comes with that suffering—cling to His promises. Listen through the silence and hear the sound of His love orchestrating all the details of your life for your good and for His glorious design.

Remember: He has spoken.

APPLY TO LIFE

Take a moment to identify any periods of intense suffering you've been through in recent years. As you think through each moment, use the space on pages 110-111 to answer the following questions:

1.   What caused your suffering in the first place?
2.   What lessened your suffering during that period?
3.   What caused you to suffer more?
4.   How have you changed in the time since that period of suffering?

Read Psalm 28 out loud during each of your daily devotions this week. Offer each word as a prayer to God, as David did thousands of years ago. When you finish, write down any phrases within the psalm that impacted you, or anything you heard from God during the prayer.

During the week, keep an eye out for anyone in your circle of friends and family who may be suffering. When you identify someone going through a rough time, start a conversation and see if there is any way you can help. Also, pray for that person throughout the week.

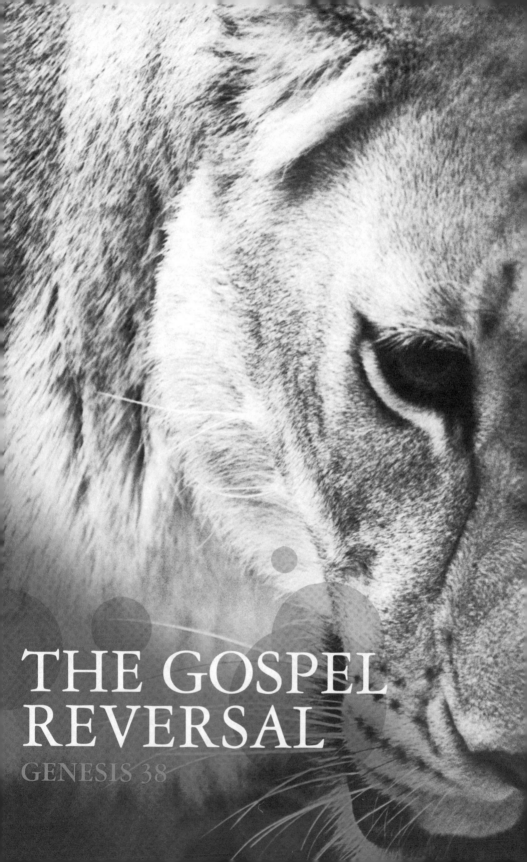

THE GOSPEL REVERSAL

GENESIS 38

SESSION SIX

"Judah, your brothers will praise you. Your hand will be on the necks of your enemies; your father's sons will bow down to you. **Judah is a young lion—** my son, you return from the kill. He crouches; he lies down like a lion or a lioness—who dares to rouse him? The scepter will not depart from Judah or the staff from between his feet until He whose right it is comes and the obedience of the peoples belongs to Him. He ties his donkey to a vine, and the colt of his donkey to the choice vine. He washes his clothes in wine and his robes in the blood of grapes. His eyes are darker than wine, and his teeth are whiter than milk" (Genesis 49:8-12).

[Spoiler alert!] Things turned out pretty great for Joseph in the end. He got the girl. He got his dream job. He restored his family. And he saved the world.

Sometimes I (Matt) envy Joseph—not because of all the cool things that happened to him in the end, but because of how he behaved when everything was going wrong. He was knocked around with every obstacle life had in its bag, but he stood firm. Sure, when he was 17 he was kind of a brat, but for the rest of his story he displayed nothing but integrity.

When I read about him, I imagine Joseph as one of those guys who are always in a good mood—always quoting Scripture verses and singing worship songs. He obeyed God in the most tempting of circumstances. He forgave his brothers without a second thought. And he took all the junk without complaining.

If I'm not careful, I can look at the outcome of Joseph's life and think: *Man, standing firm really pays off.* Sometimes I start thinking that things worked out great for Joseph because he didn't mess up—that things would have gone very differently if Joseph hadn't been so upright.

In other words, it's tempting to believe that God worked great things in Joseph's life because Joseph was such a good guy. But that's a dangerous idea.

What are your overall reactions to Joseph's story?

Why is it a dangerous idea to believe that things worked out well for Joseph because he was faithful to God?

I'm a pastor of a church. I have a staff of more than 100 people. Thousands of souls look to me for leadership every week, and I want things to turn out great. I want God to move. I want Him to work things out for our good and His glory. When hardships and suffering come, it's not hard for me to trust that God is going to prevail for our good and His glory.

But there are nights when I lay in bed seriously concerned about *me*—that my sin is going to ruin all of God's plans. There are corners of my heart that are darker than I even know, and it makes me nervous. There are times when I'm eaten up with anxiety because I believe the lie that God's ability to use me for His glory depends on my obedience.

. . . .

Listen to "Oh Great God, Give Us Rest"
by David Crowder Band from the
Creation Restored playlist, available at
threadsmedia.com/creationrestored.

That's why my favorite part of Joseph's section in Genesis isn't about Joseph at all.

A SORDID STORY

Genesis 38 interrupts Joseph's crazy life to give us a glimpse of what's going on back home in Canaan. The story zooms in on Judah, the same brother who was the brainchild behind selling Joseph to Egypt. This chapter is one of the weirdest "asides" you'll see in Scripture. I'm pretty sure it wasn't taught to you in Sunday school when you were a kid learning about Joseph—although those would have been some interesting flannelgraphs, to say the least.

Believe it or not, this story is one of the clearest depictions of the gospel we find anywhere in Scripture. That's what makes it so offensive.

> "Judah got a wife for Er, his firstborn, and her name was Tamar. Now Er, Judah's firstborn, was evil in the LORD's sight, and the LORD put him to death. Then Judah said to Onan, 'Sleep with your brother's wife. Perform your duty as her brother-in-law and produce offspring for your brother.' But Onan knew that the offspring would not be his, so whenever he slept with his brother's wife, he released his semen on the ground so that he would not produce offspring for his brother. What he did was evil in the LORD's sight, so He put him to death also" (Genesis 38:6-10).

What are your initial reactions to this passage?

Judah had three sons: Er, Onan, and Shelah. He found a wife for Er, and her name was Tamar. The two of them didn't live happily ever after, though. Er was "evil in the LORD's sight," so God put him to death.

The next bit sounds strange to us, but it was part of God's plan to provide for widows in the Israelite culture. Basically, the brother of a deceased husband was supposed to marry the widow so that she would still be able to have children and continue the name of her family. That's where Onan came in—he was sent by Judah to "perform [his] duty" so that Er's family line wouldn't die out. But Onan wasn't on board with God's plan for provision, and he refused to get Tamar pregnant. Withholding children from Tamar was also deemed "evil in the LORD's sight," so God put Onan to death, too.

Now you see why this part of Genesis usually gets skipped in Sunday School. Believe it or not, things got worse.

 Other examples of God putting people to death because of disobedience include: Genesis 6:5-7; Genesis 19:13; Acts 5:4; and 1 Corinthians 11:29-31.

For starters, Judah stopped trying to fulfill his obligation to Tamar:

> **"Then Judah said to his daughter-in-law Tamar, 'Remain a widow in your father's house until my son Shelah grows up.' For he thought, 'He might die too, like his brothers.' So Tamar went to live in her father's house (Genesis 38:11).**

This was a big deal. He disobeyed Gods's command and was culturally unfair to his daughter-in-law. Still, we can understand the motivation behind Judah's decision. The man had lost two sons, and instead of realizing that his sons' actions were the problem, he irrationally placed the blame for those losses on Tamar.

But then things got weird:

> **"Tamar was told, 'Your father-in-law is going up to Timnah to shear his sheep.' So she took off her widow's clothes, veiled her face, covered herself, and sat at the entrance to Enaim, which is on the way to Timnah. For she saw that, though Shelah had grown up, she had not been given to him as a wife. When Judah saw her, he thought she was a prostitute, for she had covered her face. He went over to her and said, 'Come, let me sleep with you,' for he did not know that she was his daughter-in-law" (vv. 13-16).**

To make a long story short, Tamar did sleep with Judah—after taking his signet ring, cord, and staff as a kind of "promise to pay." And to make things even more complicated, she became pregnant with Judah's child.

Again, Tamar's actions weren't correct, but there were some mitigating circumstances that help us understand why she tricked her father-in-law into sleeping with her and getting her pregnant. She had lost two husbands, for starters. She was a single woman in a man's world; she had been betrayed and abandoned by the people God had appointed to provide for her.

Not that Judah considered any of that when he first heard the news:

> **"About three months later Judah was told, 'Your daughter-in-law, Tamar, has been acting like a prostitute, and now she is pregnant.'**
>
> **"'Bring her out!' Judah said. 'Let her be burned to death!'**
>
> **"As she was being brought out, she sent her father-in-law this message:**

 "You are not to have sexual intercourse with your daughter-in-law. She is your son's wife; you are not to have sex with her" (Leviticus 18:15).

"'I am pregnant by the man to whom these items belong.' And she added, 'Examine them. Whose signet ring, cord, and staff are these?'

"Judah recognized them and said, 'She is more in the right than I, since I did not give her to my son Shelah.' And he did not know her intimately again" (vv. 24-26).

By the end of these verses we're made to understand that Tamar was not the villain in this story. She wasn't blameless, but she was "more in the right" than Judah. For his part, Judah didn't react with violence or denial when he learned the truth. He repented.

Basically, the whole soap-opera situation boiled down to two sinful people who made mistakes. That makes sense, but it still leaves us with several questions: Why is this story in the Bible? What are we supposed to learn from it? And what in the world does it have to do with the gospel?

How would you answer those questions right now?

What other questions do you have about the story of Judah and Tamar?

JOSEPH VS. JUDAH

There are good answers to those questions. In order to get at them, we need to take a step back and look at the broader picture in this section of Genesis.

Genesis 37 tells the story of Joseph being betrayed by his brothers, sold, and sent to Egypt as a slave. Chapter 38 narrows the lens to focus on one of those brothers, Judah, who had an illicit affair with his daughter-in-law. Chapter 39 picks up the story of Joseph again, including the moment when he refused to have an affair with Potiphar's wife (and was thrown in prison because of it).

Moses, the author of Genesis, directly compares Judah and Joseph. When we read their stories back-to-back, the contrast between their moral character and actions is revealed.

That's bad news for Judah, because Joseph was a stand-up guy. Even though he started out a little snooty, Joseph became the type of person most of us want to be. In comparison, Judah was the "bad boy." He was the black sheep in the family of promise.

So here's a question: If God put Joseph and Judah in front of us and told us to pick one of them to be a direct means of ushering in the salvation of the world, who would we pick?

We'd pick Joseph, of course. We'd pick the guy with the better resumé, impeccable morals, and obvious leadership potential. Certainly we wouldn't pick the guy who tried to kill his brother—the guy who turned his back on his daughter-in-law and slept with prostitutes.

The only problem is that God so often seems to pick the wrong person.

We've already seen God choose the younger brother over the older several times in Genesis. We've seen Him choose Abraham the moon-worshiper and Jacob the deceiver. Later in the Bible we see God pick guys like David, a lowly shepherd and an adulterer. We see Him set His favor on Paul, a murderer, and Peter, a heretic and traitor.

How do you react to this list of "black sheep"?

Where else in Scripture does God pick the "wrong" person to do His work?

We would pick Joseph, but God picked Judah.

The Book of Matthew opens with a genealogy of our Savior. It lists "the historical record of Jesus Christ, the Son of David, the Son of Abraham" (1:1). And look who's listed among Jesus' ancestors:

> **"Abraham fathered Isaac, Isaac fathered Jacob, Jacob fathered Judah and his brothers, Judah fathered Perez and Zerah by Tamar, Perez fathered Hezron, Hezron fathered Aram" (Matthew 1:2-3).**

When Matthew recounts the fathers of the faith, it's Judah, not Joseph, whose name joins Abraham's, Isaac's, and Jacob's. When Matthew recounts the heritage of Jesus, it's Judah whose name is called out. Jesus is the Lion of the tribe of Judah (see Revelation 5:5).

More than that, Jesus comes from this story right here in Genesis 38. It's this unorthodox, disturbing, deceitful intimacy between Judah and Tamar that produced Perez. And it's Perez who was the ancestor of David and, ultimately, Jesus.

Watch the *Creation Restored* video "The Gospel Reversal," available at *threadsmedia.com/creationrestored.*

That's not as big of a deal to our postmodern sensibilities. It may even seem cool—Jesus came from the wrong side of the tracks. But in the Israelite culture, family was identity. The Israelites likely saw Judah and Tamar listed in that genealogy and thought: *Couldn't God have picked a better family? Couldn't He have picked a better heritage for Jesus? Why does God parade this humiliating account around as if He's proud of the evil and wickedness in His Son's family history?*

God sees things differently than us. He sees sin differently. He sees righteousness differently, and He sees salvation differently.

GOD SEES SIN DIFFERENTLY THAN US

We brushed over something at the beginning of Genesis 38 that deserves a second look. Remember Er and Onan, Judah's oldest sons? The text says that both of them were "evil in the LORD's sight." As a result, God killed them both—just dropped them dead. Boom.

The God present in those verses is a stranger to many of us. We don't know Him. Our God would never strike people dead for something as small as refusing to obey His plan for a widow's provision. Our God would never kill 2 guys in 10 verses.

The only problem is that our God did. It's written down in Genesis.

God Sees Sin as Serious

The God of these verses is indeed the Christian God. He's the only God. The sweet Father who holds you in His arms and comforts you in the midst of your suffering is the same Person who killed two men in the blink of an eye.

He did it so we might know He sees sin differently from us. He wanted to show us a glimpse of His holiness and the severity with which He approaches sin.

We typically see sin as an inconvenience—an irritating part of our flesh. If we're lucky, we have moments when sin seems like a burden and a weight. Every now and then we glimpse the gravity of our sin and the offense of our rebellion against a holy God. Yet even in our best moments we think God's response to sin is like killing a fly with a machine gun. In the depths of our hearts we suppress the truth in unrighteousness and believe the lie that God's behavior in passages like this is an overreaction.

Because we see sin so differently from God—because we so drastically underestimate the severity of the issue—we can't understand stories like the death of Er and Onan. We're shocked by those who died, when we should be shocked by those allowed to live.

 A prostitute named Rahab is also part of Jesus' genealogy. You can read her story in Joshua 2.

The more we grasp the terrifying consequences of sin, the more clearly we'll see the gospel. Sin is so horrific that God had to pour out wrath on His own Son just to let you and me stand in His presence.

If you know of places in your life where you have a hard time grasping the seriousness of sin, spend some time meditating on the cross. The cross wasn't just a random act of kindness from a God of love; it wasn't just a display of His great mercy. The punishment Christ endured on the cross was the penalty for our sin. The cross is a picture of just how big a deal sin is to God.

God Sees Sin as Deserving of Punishment

Even when we begin to understand that God takes a serious view of sin in general, we still think that being a Christian puts a little asterisk by our names. We see the horror of God's response to sin, but we calm ourselves with the news that it's different for us—that God doesn't care about *our* sin because we're in Christ.

Again, the problem with that line of thinking is the Bible. God's Word was written for God's people. It was designed to have power and impact in the lives of God's children. Meaning, God had Christians in mind when He highlighted His hatred of sin in this passage.

He highlighted it for you.

Do you feel like God punishes you for your sin? Why or why not?

There are two kinds of peace we can feel about our sin. One is the peace that comes from trusting Jesus for our righteousness. The other is the peace that comes from falsely telling ourselves that God doesn't care about our sin or that we're really not that bad. Only the first leads to life.

We can tell which type of peace we have by looking at the way we respond to texts like Genesis 38. If our right-standing with God is found in Christ, then looking at our sin doesn't make us uncomfortable. Meditating on the gravity of our sin and the just consequence of death doesn't threaten us because we know the debt has been paid.

However, if our peace is not founded in the gospel reversal, then we'll look at these verses and feel threatened. We'll feel like we're being condemned. Or we'll skip them altogether thinking they don't apply to us.

 "God is none other than the Saviour of our wretchedness. So we can only know God well by knowing our iniquities.... Those who have known God, without knowing their wretchedness, have not glorified him, but have glorified themselves." —Blaise Pascal[1]

When we see the way God responded to the wickedness of Judah's sons, we should remember that every one of our sins must also be met with death. There isn't a gospel loophole.

The only difference for followers of Christ is that He has stepped in and taken the punishment for us.

God Sees Sin as an Opportunity

We also take a misguided view of sin when we see it as something that ruins our lives and trashes God's plans for us. That's because God sees sin as an opportunity to set the stage for His glory to shine.

There was a reason God picked Judah and not Joseph to be the Messiah's ancestor. He did it because using "sinners" and broken people to do His will makes much of His strength.

Think about it: There's no risk of Judah robbing glory from God because of his righteousness and wisdom. Rather, people look at everything God accomplished through Judah and instantly know that God alone gets the credit.

God picked Judah for the same reason He picked Moses—the guy who had a speech impediment to be His mouthpiece. Why would He do that? Because God doesn't see things as we do. God sees the weak and the sick as an opportunity to display the greatness of His healing power.

> **"Brothers, consider your calling: Not many are wise from a human perspective, not many powerful, not many of noble birth. Instead, God has chosen what is foolish in the world to shame the wise, and God has chosen what is weak in the world to shame the strong. God has chosen what is insignificant and despised in the world—what is viewed as nothing—to bring to nothing what is viewed as something, so that no one can boast in His presence" (1 Corinthians 1:26-29).**

God doesn't take sin lightly. God doesn't act as if sin doesn't matter. But God does redeem sinners. No sin is darker or deeper than the grace of God.

Sometimes I think about what it'll be like to see Joseph in heaven. When we hear God read out the details of Joseph's life—all the ways He was glorified through Joseph's obedience— it's going to be great. The angels will worship God for His ability to change hearts. The saints will praise God for the way Joseph's life testifies that God is better than selfish gain. The obedience in Joseph's life will cause us all to sing of God's faithfulness for years.

Listen to "Shame" by Fernando Ortega from the *Creation Restored* playlist, available at *threadsmedia.com/creationunraveled.*

Then I think about Judah. And I think it's going to be great to see him, too. We'll stand there as God reads out the many failures in Judah's life—all the dark corners in his heart and all the ways he failed to live up to the standard of righteousness. And then we'll all sing of Christ and His blood. We'll sing about how God's mercy and grace runs deeper than we dreamed. We'll sing about the blood that is more powerful than we imagined and how it can redeem the darkest hearts.

Make no mistake: God will get glory out of His children, whether through sunshine or sin. Even when we mess up, even when we turn away, even when we don't do what we're supposed to—we don't have the power to sabotage the glory of God.

GOD SEES RIGHTEOUSNESS DIFFERENTLY THAN US

Look again at Judah's conclusion after the whole incident with Tamar:

> "Judah recognized them and said, 'She is more in the right than I, since I did not give her to my son Shelah.' And he did not know her intimately again" (Genesis 38:26).

That phrase "in the right" is often translated as "righteous," which is a church word that really refers to a person's goodness. In the Bible, a righteous person is someone who is good enough to stand before God. In our contemporary culture, a righteous person is someone who is "good enough," period.

As we'll see, our vision of what makes someone good and God's vision of what makes someone good are radically different.

We define righteousness as avoiding the big sins and doing good things instead. And by that standard, we can see clearly that Judah is not a righteous guy. We know that because he tried to kill his brother and he slept with a prostitute. No one looks at Judah and tries to defend him as righteous.

But what's fascinating about this story is that the biggest mistake—the sin that led Judah to repentance and the moment around which the entire story hinges—is not Judah's hatred for his brother or his interactions with a prostitute. The failure in this story occurred when Judah placed the safety of his son over the will of God.

Let that rest on you for a second. The "big" sin in this passage happened when a broken father put the safety of his kid above God's will. The "big" sin was a man seeking to protect his own son at the expense of a widow.

God had a smorgasbord of things to take issue with in Judah's life, but He highlighted the sin of neglecting a widow in need, and He did it intentionally. He did it because He wanted us to see righteousness differently. He wanted us to know that righteousness isn't just avoiding "big" sins and doing good deeds. The standard of righteousness is that in every moment, in every way, we put the will of God above our desires.

If we wake up in the morning and read our Bible and make our spouse breakfast and go to work and smile at our coworkers and make it through the day without getting drunk or sleeping around or yelling at anyone—we think we're doing pretty good. But none of these things make us righteous.

The Bible's standard for righteousness is that we love God and exalt His glory at all times:

> **"Love the Lord your God with all your heart, with all your soul, and with all your mind. This is the greatest and most important command"** (Matthew 22:37-38).

Those were Jesus' words. When He was asked about the greatest commandment, He didn't respond by telling the people to perform or avoid certain actions. He told them that the standard of righteousness is to love God with everything they had.

The root of Judah's unrighteousness wasn't sleeping with a prostitute. It wasn't even neglecting a widow. Those were just symptoms. The root was that he didn't love God with everything in him. He loved his child more than he loved God. He loved sex more than he loved God.

God wants us to see that our vision of righteousness is skewed, as well. Have we ever put the safety of our kids above the will of God? Have we ever put our own safety above His will? Have we ever ignored His revealed plan for our lives because we wanted to protect our financial or physical or emotional well-being?

We've all done it a million times. We do it every time we're anxious about something—God said not to worry, but we ignore His command because our well-being matters more to us than His will. We do it every time we have a lustful thought. We do it every time we plan our budgets without consulting Him.

A better question would be: Have we ever had a moment when we didn't love God with every part of our being? Have we ever had a single second when we weren't worshiping God with all of our faculties?

Leading a group? It's the way to go. Find extra questions and teaching tools in the leader kit, available at *threadsmedia.com/creationrestored.*

If we answer yes to those questions—and we all must answer yes—then we're disqualified from the title of "righteous."

The Bible is clear:

> "There is no one righteous, not even one. There is no one who understands; there is no one who seeks God. All have turned away; all alike have become useless. There is no one who does what is good, not even one" (Romans 3:10-12).

That passage is talking about us. We're all wicked. We all fit the description of a crime that God decreed in Genesis 38 to be worthy of instant death.

What happened to Judah's sons wasn't shocking when we see sin and righteousness the way God does. And when we do, we'll prepare ourselves to finally see the gospel as good news. That's because understanding how far we are from righteousness doesn't take us further from salvation; it draws us nearer to salvation.

The heart that recognizes its failure is closer to God than ever before.

This is the gospel reversal. Nothing is more offensive to the arrogance of the American dream than the idea that we aren't good enough, we're failures, and we can't work our way out of the "wicked" category. It goes against everything we've been taught about self-esteem.

But the great gospel reversal says that the beginning of peace is the awareness that we're failures before God.

GOD SEES SALVATION DIFFERENTLY THAN US

Whether we would say it or not, most of us believe in karma. We believe in some sort of cosmic scale where our good deeds are weighed against our bad. We think that if we have more good than bad, we should be saved.

We believe that good people should go to heaven. Most of us know better than to say it out loud—especially around other church people—but it's there in the corners of our hearts. It's there when we get confused about someone who keeps failing God and keeps receiving blessings. It's there when we get bitter at God for giving us hard times even though we've been doing everything "right." It's there when we read our Bibles out of fear that God will send us a bad day if we don't. It's there when we pray harder or repent repeatedly or go to church more to try to make up for a bad season with God.

....

 "For all have sinned and fall short of the glory of God. They are justified freely by His grace through the redemption that is in Christ Jesus" (Romans 3:23-24).

It's there when we're bewildered by bad things happening to good people. It's there when we're angered by good things happening to bad people.

In our hearts, we believe that doing good works will get us closer to God. Deep down, we believe that what we do affects how God feels about us. We think our actions can make Him love us more or less.

In other words, we don't see salvation the way God does.

Do you agree with these statements? Why or why not?

Which of these descriptions connect with any of your recent thoughts or concerns?

God calls us to concede that we're wicked. He calls us to see the great gospel reversal, where He blesses those who join Judah in proclaiming their own wickedness.

When you think about it, the Bible is one big story about good things happening to bad people. And the story of Judah, just like every story in this Bible, tells us the gospel.

What did Judah deserve? Death. God spent the first 11 verses of the chapter making that clear. But God didn't leave it there. He let a right view of sin and righteousness set the stage to display a right view of salvation. He let the horror of sin and Judah's unrighteousness be the dark backdrop that displayed the glory of His mercy and grace.

God didn't kill Judah, but that's not the end of the story. He didn't just spare the sinner, He *blessed* the sinner. He used Judah's brokenness to bring forth the great King David and the greatest King Jesus.

Here's God's view of salvation: His saving grace and favor doesn't get set on those who consider themselves "good." It gets set on the screw-ups. And that's the gospel. God chose the sick, the weak, and the wounded of this world and not only spared them, but blessed them. He saved sinners from death by punishing His Son.

That's why we can look at the horror of our sin without fear. We can fully embrace that we're truly dark creatures, and yet we can still be filled with hope and peace because our sin has been paid in full.

GOD SEES SUCCESS DIFFERENTLY THAN US

For God, success involves displaying His character and glory most clearly. That's why He so often chooses to work through sinners.

Success for God is doing whatever it takes to have all His children find their hope in Christ's resumé alone. His goal for our lives is that we stand more fully on Christ in every moment— that every good thing coming out of our lives would trace back to Christ in us.

The mark of success in the life of a believer isn't avoiding failure; it isn't even doing good things. Success in the life of a believer is becoming more and more dependent on Christ at every turn. It's needing and pointing to Him as the only hope of our salvation and sanctification. It's using our failure to display our trust in Him. We call that repentance.

Unfortunately, we often see success as independence. In our minds, the more we mature in Christ, the less we'll need Him. We view success as taking the blank slate bought for us by the blood of Christ and building a better resumé than the one we had before.

We look at Joseph as an example of success—we'd love to have his testimony. But at the end of the day, Judah's story was just as successful as Joseph's. Judah may not have done everything right, but because God set His favor on Judah, he had the mark of success. His repentance displayed God's character and glory.

What has been your standard for success in life? What are you shooting for?

What are some things God labels as "failure" in the lives of His followers?

We get another picture of success and failure in Luke 22, where Jesus addressed Peter for one of the last times before Peter's betrayal. Jesus said:

> **"Simon, Simon, look out! Satan has asked to sift you like wheat. But I have prayed for you that your faith may not fail. And you, when you have turned back, strengthen your brothers" (Luke 22:31-32).**

Jesus' prayer was specific. He prayed that Peter's faith wouldn't fail, and He prayed that when Peter had "turned back," he'd be used to strengthen others. But just a few hours after Peter heard this, he denied Jesus three times. That sure looks like a failure of faith to me!

 A 2009 survey from the Barna Group revealed that 81 percent of teens expect to have a "great-paying" job by the time they turn 25. Also, 80 percent expect to have a job where they can "make a difference."[2]

We have two options: Either Jesus' prayer didn't work, or Peter's faith didn't fail. Thankfully, the second option represents the truth.

This text makes it clear that failure of faith is different from a moment of sin. Even though Peter made a series of terrible mistakes, he didn't let go of his faith—which was the crux of Jesus' prayer. Rather, Peter "turned back" and repented of his sin.

Judas and Peter both denied Jesus, but we view them so differently. We love one and detest the other. And yet, just like Esau and Jacob, there's only one marked difference between Peter and Judas: One repented, and the other didn't.

Think about the similarities between Peter, Jacob, and Judah. They were all given the mark of God's favor, but it didn't show up in the form of sinless lives. Rather, it showed up as the gift of repentance.

As crazy as it may sound, followers of Jesus should be more desperate for repentance like Judah's than testimonies like Joseph's.

How do you react to that statement?

What does it take to develop a life of repentance?

Let's gets one thing straight before moving on: It's good to obey God and resist sin. Joseph's life makes that clear. It's good to fear disobedience. It's good to stay awake at night plotting purity and clinging to the hope of victory over sin. That's a powerful testimony.

However, we need to desire hearts that trust God more than we desire temporary victories over sin. And according to God's Word, repentance is the road to that kind of success.

The failure we should fear most isn't the failure of external sin, but the failure of an unrepentant heart. The thing we should fear most isn't our sin, but our inability to repent.

We should rejoice, therefore, whenever we notice some outburst of sin in our lives. That sin has been there all the time, lurking beneath the surface. But those moments when we realize it and recognize it are gracious evidences that God is working in us to give us opportunities to repent.

In order for that to work, however, we still need to grasp the first part of Genesis 38. We need to grasp the seriousness of sin and the consequences it carries. If we can't understand the seriousness of sin—our sin, specifically—then we'll never repent.

We must find ourselves like Judah: Broken over the moments in our lives when we chose temporary comforts over God's will. We must let those moments break us. We must meditate on the seriousness of our sin and the lack of righteousness in our lives, and we must worship God for His view of salvation and success that makes such sin the beginning, not the end, of our stories.

REPENTANCE AND REST

There was much tragedy in Jacob's family, but also so much hidden hope. There must have been days when Jacob looked at his sons with a heavy heart. After all his attempts to shield them from his failure and mistakes, they seemed destined to destroy the great lineage God had promised to provide. Think of all the failure represented by those men. Think of all the sin and sorrow in one family.

And yet, out of all the people in all the world, God set His favor on that family. He never left them—not even when they seemed to do everything in their power to disrupt His plans for their lives.

The reason is simple: God is faithful to Himself. He made a promise to Abraham one starry night, and nothing in heaven and earth could shake the sureness of His word. He won't forsake us, either. He had us in mind when He ordained these stories. He had us in mind when He brought Joseph to Egypt through Judah's evil intentions. He had us in mind when He brought life into Tamar's womb through a disturbing sexual encounter.

He had a plan for us then, He has a plan for us now, and nothing can shake that plan. Nothing can shake His promise to provide for and protect us. Sometimes we don't believe that. Sometimes we wonder if God could still be on our side even after all we've done against Him. Could God still be for those of us who seek to shipwreck His plan at every turn?

Yes. Just as suffering is a certainty in this life, so is failure. If we have eyes to see it, we can look at our lives today and identify a million ways we've already failed to live up to God's standard. We've already rejected Him, ignored Him, and forsaken Him.

And tomorrow we'll wake up and do it all again.

The great news is that the gospel is as real today as it was the first time we heard it. God's light is most clearly displayed in darkness. His righteousness is most clearly seen in our wickedness—His strength in our weakness and His faithfulness in our faithlessness.

God's salvation and success are most clearly seen when they're held up against the backdrop of our sin and unrighteousness.

I like what the prophet Isaiah wrote:

> **"For the Lord God, the Holy One of Israel, has said: 'You will be delivered by returning and resting; your strength will lie in quiet confidence. But you are not willing'" (Isaiah 30:15).**

That is success for God: repentance and rest.

Like Judah, we can lift up our faces to heaven and proclaim that we have done what is wrong in God's eyes. We can know with all our hearts that we deserve death. And we can be certain that God will give us grace because Jesus has taken our punishment, and through His sacrifice He has made us good.

We can view salvation and success the same way God does. We can repent and rest in the finished work of Christ.

APPLY TO LIFE

Take some time this week to read about three more biblical characters who made big mistakes. As you read about their failures, also make sure to note what contributions these people made to the kingdom of God.

- Moses (read Numbers 20:1-13 and Deuteronomy 34)
- David (read 2 Samuel 11-12)
- Peter (read Matthew 26:69-75)

Because God is serious about sin, confession and repentance are vital practices for His followers. This week, make an effort to confess your sins to a close friend or spouse—maybe even set up an accountability relationship with that person. Remember what the Scriptures say in James 5:16: "Therefore, confess your sins to one another and pray for one another, so that you may be healed. The urgent request of a righteous person is very powerful in its effect."

THE GOD WHO SETS US FREE

GENESIS 39–50

SESSION SEVEN

"Then I heard a loud voice from the throne: Look! God's dwelling is with humanity, and He will live with them. They will be His people, and God Himself will be with them and be their God. He will wipe away every tear from their eyes. Death will no longer exist; grief, crying, and pain will exist no longer, because the previous things have passed away" (Revelation 21:3-4).

The Bible is filled with verses and stories that proclaim God's goodness and sovereignty. The Scriptures declare the truth that God is absolutely good and absolutely in control over all things—including the suffering and evil in the world.

All Christians are on board with the part about God's goodness. We get that. But many people remain unsure about the doctrine of sovereignty. Some fear that such a doctrine promotes apathy in evangelism and a lukewarm fight against sin. Others worry that it turns believers against one another and prevents seekers from running to God's embrace.

Maybe that's how you feel. Maybe thinking about the concept of God's sovereignty makes you uncomfortable.

We can address those reservations by exploring Joseph's life. His story shows that what we believe about God's purposes in the world affects every aspect of our lives; it shows the great freedom that's possible for those who believe in God's goodness and sovereign rule.

That's right: freedom and sovereignty can go together. We often think of God's sovereignty as a chain around our necks. We think that if God has total control over everything in our lives, we are not free to do anything. That's a lie. As we'll explore throughout this session, God's sovereignty frees us to become the people we were created to be.

FREE TO PURSUE HOLINESS

When we reconnect with Joseph at the beginning of Genesis 39, an Egyptian named Potiphar had bought him as a slave from the Ishmaelites. We're told that Joseph worked hard in Potiphar's house, and he was eventually put in charge of everything his master owned. Things were looking up.

The problem was Joseph's physique. He was a good-looking man, and it didn't take long before somebody noticed:

> "After some time his master's wife looked longingly at Joseph and said, 'Sleep with me.' But he refused. 'Look,' he said to his master's wife, 'with me here my master does not concern himself with anything in his house, and he has put all that he owns under my authority. No one in this house is greater than I am. He has withheld nothing from me except you, because you are his wife. So how could I do such a great evil and sin against God?'

> "Although she spoke to Joseph day after day, he refused to go to bed with her" (Genesis 39:7-10).

Listen to "Christ Has Set Me Free" by Rend Collective Experiment from the *Creation Restored* playlist, available at *threadsmedia.com/creationrestored*.

Joseph's integrity in that situation was impressive. After being betrayed, abandoned, and forced into an unwanted life, he still pursued holiness without hesitation. He could remain faithful in that pursuit because he held on to a deep belief in the sovereignty and goodness of God. We know this because of what he said.

Most people have been impacted by adultery within their circles of friends and family, or at least they've seen it on TV. We usually react by saying, "How could she do that to him after so many years?" or "How could a man do that to his wife after all she gave him?"

Joseph said something different. He mentioned his master's trust, but he didn't say, "How could I do such a great evil and sin against my master?" He said, "How could I do such a great evil and sin against God?"

That little switch means everything. In effect, Joseph said: "I believe God is in control of my life, and I believe He's good. So why should I take something He hasn't given to me? I don't want to testify that God is withholding anything from me." Joseph was free to pursue holiness because he believed God had given him everything.

Think back to Genesis 3—the root of sin. Adam and Eve were in the same situation as Joseph. God had literally given them paradise, but there was one thing He told them they couldn't have. Adam and Eve ate the forbidden fruit because they didn't trust God's sovereign, good provision in their lives. They sinned because they thought He was either holding out on them in cruelty or unable to give them what they needed.

What other similarities and differences can you find between Joseph's temptation and the temptation of Adam and Eve?

We've all failed. We've all sinned. While it may seem that we primarily sin against our spouses, friends, coworkers, employers, and strangers, the truth is that every sin creeping out of the dark corners of our hearts is a rebellion against God. Our sin is a result of our unbelief in God's goodness and sovereignty.

When we jealously compare ourselves to others, we reflect a doubt that God has given us what's best. When we glance lustfully at our computers, get angry at our coworkers, or perform self-righteous good deeds, we reflect a heart that doesn't firmly believe God is working all things for our good and His glory.

Those moments of failure are going to come, but we can limit their impact in our lives by pursuing holiness, as Joseph did.

 "Then the woman saw that the tree was good for food and delightful to look at, and that it was desirable for obtaining wisdom. So she took some of its fruit and ate it; she also gave some to her husband, who was with her, and he ate it" (Genesis 3:6).

In what areas of life (work, home, church, school, etc.) do you find it easiest to pursue holiness?

In what areas of life do you have the most trouble pursuing holiness? Why?

If we trust that God is good, we'll have the faith to pursue holiness no matter how difficult the situation or how powerful the temptation. If we can wrap our hearts around the idea that God is in control—that He is sovereign—even in the valleys, then we won't fall into the trap of thinking we have to take things into our own hands.

When Satan whispers the lie that we'll miss out if we walk in purity, we can look right back at him with full assurance that God has both the heart and the strength to make sure no good thing is withheld from those who walk uprightly.

FREE TO SUFFER WELL

One day, Potiphar's wife found Joseph in the house without any of the other servants around. She decided to take things to the next level:

> "She grabbed him by his garment and said, 'Sleep with me!' But leaving his garment in her hand, he escaped and ran outside. When she saw that he had left his garment with her and had run outside, she called the household servants. 'Look,' she said to them, 'my husband brought a Hebrew man to make fools of us. He came to me so he could sleep with me, and I screamed as loud as I could. When he heard me screaming for help, he left his garment with me and ran outside'" (Genesis 39:12-15).

When Potiphar heard about the attack, he became furious. He threw Joseph in prison without any kind of trial or due process.

When have you been punished for making the right choice? What was the outcome?

Joseph's pursuit of purity cost him everything he'd worked to build after being sold as a slave. Yet not once in the text do we see him become angry or cry out to God at the injustice of his imprisonment.

 A survey conducted in 2007 by the Pew Research Center found that 38 percent of adults view pre-marital sex as always or almost always wrong.[1]

Rather, Joseph was free to suffer persecution without fear or anger because He knew that God is kind and in control. Even in a place like prison, even after being unjustly accused, Joseph knew God was with him:

> "But the LORD was with Joseph and extended kindness to him. He granted him favor in the eyes of the prison warden. The warden put all the prisoners who were in the prison under Joseph's authority, and he was responsible for everything that was done there. The warden did not bother with anything under Joseph's authority, because the LORD was with him, and the LORD made everything that he did successful" (Genesis 39:21-23).

"The LORD was with Joseph and extended kindness to him." That's a strange phrase, given the context. If God really wanted to show kindness to Joseph, couldn't He have done so by keeping him out of prison?

No, God chose a different path. He showed Joseph His steadfast love not by saving him *from* some of the worst years of his life—not by protecting him *from* unjust accusations—but by walking *with* Joseph in the midst of those struggles and ordaining the details of those tragic years.

So often we beg for God to "show up" in the midst of our difficult situations, but what we really want is for God to rescue us from trials. When we ask God to be present in our lives, we really want Him to deliver us from suffering. We miss the truth that God has already showed up in our lives. He's delivering us through suffering.

We need to heed the words of the apostle Peter:

> "Dear friends, don't be surprised when the fiery ordeal comes among you to test you as if something unusual were happening to you. Instead, rejoice as you share in the sufferings of the Messiah, so that you may also rejoice with great joy at the revelation of His glory" (1 Peter 4:12-13).

Don't be surprised when suffering comes. Trust that God is good and in control:

> "So those who suffer according to God's will should, while doing what is good, entrust themselves to a faithful Creator" (1 Peter 4:19).

That's what happened with Joseph. He ended up in prison for a crime he didn't commit. He suffered, not because God didn't love him, not even in spite of the fact that God loved him, but *because* God loved him.

FREE TO CONSIDER OTHERS

Meanwhile, there was some drama going on in the palace. Two servants offended Pharaoh, and they were both thrown into the same prison as Joseph. We're told in the text that they "were in custody for some time," and that the warden assigned Joseph to be their personal attendant (Genesis 40:1-4).

One night, both of Pharaoh's servants had disturbing dreams that left them shaken in the morning. Read what happened next:

> **"When Joseph came to them in the morning, he saw that they looked distraught. So he asked Pharaoh's officers who were in custody with him in his master's house, 'Why do you look so sad today?'**
>
> **"'We had dreams,' they said to him, 'but there is no one to interpret them.'**
>
> **"Then Joseph said to them, 'Don't interpretations belong to God? Tell me your dreams'" (Genesis 40:6-8).**

Notice the difference from the Joseph we saw at the beginning of his story. Somewhere along the way, that cocky 17-year-old bragging about his dreams became a man who saw God as the center of every story.

Joseph also found a new kind of humility. He wasn't just thinking less of himself; he was thinking of himself less. The two servants didn't approach Joseph for assistance when they were troubled by their dreams. Rather, Joseph noticed their distress, and he approached them out of a desire to help.

For most of us, experiencing tragedy and challenging circumstances results in a downward spiral so strong that we become unaware of anyone else around us. Why was Joseph different? What was it about Joseph's heart that enabled him to not only notice others despite his circumstances but genuinely seek to serve them?

Joseph believed God was directing his steps with a kind and sovereign hand. That belief freed Joseph to see his imprisonment not as an obstacle, but as an opportunity. It freed Joseph to consider others even when he was in need of help.

A few years ago I (Halim) lost my mom to cancer. And it was rough. I kept finding rogue thoughts in my heart. Things like: *Why do other people get to have their moms? That person doesn't even value his mom! That kid gets to spend every weekend with her grandmother, and my kid will never know his.*

....

 Watch the *Creation Unraveled* video
"The God Who Sets Us Free," available
at *threadsmedia.com/creationrestored.*

Maybe that's part of grief, or maybe it was just my selfish heart. Either way, the more I thought about what I was missing, the more I became consumed with myself and my pain.

But as I began to feel God's sovereign goodness, I became more and more free to consider others. When I trusted God with the pieces of my pain and sorrow, I saw that I had lost a mom, but so had my sister and my wife. I saw that my dad had lost the bride of his youth. I was no longer as consumed with myself because God was taking care of me. I then became free to care for others.

And the more I thought of others, the more I experienced healing.

What difficult circumstances are preventing you from considering others?

How could God's sovereignty and goodness impact those situations?

At the center of our self-obsession is a deep fear that if we don't fight for ourselves, no one else will. We don't care for others because we're too busy advocating for ourselves.

We have to resist that impulse. We have to trust the Advocate we have already. We have to believe that He's willing and able to intervene on our behalf.

FREE TO ACT

Sometimes we think that trusting in God's sovereignty means we can stop taking action. We wouldn't say so out loud, but we view God being in control as an excuse to stop moving forward and stop valuing obedience.

We think: *If God is sovereign over sin, suffering, and everything else, then it doesn't really matter what we do. So why do anything?*

But that's not what we see in Joseph's life.

Despite his crazy circumstances, Joseph worked with all his heart at whatever was set in front of him. Why? Because he believed God was for him, and he believed God was in control. That belief freed Joseph to take action rather than searching for signs or wallowing in self-pity.

In addition, Joseph prospered because he took action. Yes, God was with him, and it was God who made all his work succeed. But we have to see that Joseph's prosperity didn't happen regardless of his actions. God worked *through* Joseph's actions to bring him good.

Here's the truth: A heart that focuses all day, every day on trusting God will take action. That heart will fearlessly move forward in faith, even when there's no writing on the wall. That heart will work hard without worrying about what might be happening in the next room. That heart will pursue holiness, even if obedience leads to persecution. That heart will look to the interests of others without concern for self-exaltation—all while trusting that God is working out the details.

If we want to discern whether we really trust God's promises, we need only look at our lives. Are they marked by hard work, the pursuit of holiness, and the humble consideration of others? Or are they marked by inaction and selfish ambition?

How would you answer the questions above?

Which of your recent actions are you most proud of? Why?

FREE TO RECEIVE GOOD

Believe it or not, living as a follower of God doesn't mean only hardship and hard work. God also blesses us with good things and good times. And when we have faith in God's goodness and sovereignty, we can accept the good moments in life without hesitation or fear.

That's something we see in the complicated interactions between Joseph, his brothers, and Jacob near the end of Genesis. In order to highlight that principle at work, we'll first need to move quickly through those interactions by summarizing several chapters in the text.

A Long Story

As we explored in session five, Joseph eventually escaped from the cycle of suffering.

After interpreting Pharaoh's dreams and offering wise counsel on how to deal with the upcoming famine, Joseph rose to second-in-command over all of Egypt. It was his job to collect grain and supplies during the seven years before the famine, and then to distribute the extra during the famine itself.

 "Whatever you do, do it enthusiastically, as something done for the Lord and not for men, knowing that you will receive the reward of an inheritance from the Lord. You serve the Lord Christ" (Colossians 3:24-25).

And that's how he came to see his brothers again, more than 20 years after they betrayed him, beat him, sold him, and sent him to Egypt as a slave.

> "The sons of Israel were among those who came to buy grain, for the famine was in the land of Canaan. Joseph was in charge of the country; he sold grain to all its people. His brothers came and bowed down before him with their faces to the ground" (Genesis 42:5-6).

There are no bold punctuation marks or capital letters in the text to alert us that something big was going down. But this was a significant moment—both in Joseph's life and the overall story of Genesis. This was the moment Joseph's dreams had predicted all those years ago. This was the moment he always knew was coming. By human standards, this was also the moment for Joseph to take his revenge or to at least deliver the ultimate "I told you so!"

However, Joseph had changed during his time in Egypt. Not only was God at work *for* Joseph, He was at work *in* Joseph. So, instead of taking revenge against his brothers, Joseph initiated an experiment to see if they'd changed.

He started by accusing the brothers of being spies, and he told them they must do something in order to prove their honesty:

> "'If you are honest, let one of you be confined to the guardhouse, while the rest of you go and take grain to relieve the hunger of your households. Bring your youngest brother to me so that your words can be confirmed; then you won't die.' And they consented to this" (Genesis 42:19-20).

Benjamin was that "youngest brother." Like Joseph, he had been born to Rachel and was a favorite of his father, Jacob. What happened next is interesting:

> "Then they said to each other, 'Obviously, we are being punished for what we did to our brother. We saw his deep distress when he pleaded with us, but we would not listen. That is why this trouble has come to us.' But Reuben replied: 'Didn't I tell you not to harm the boy? But you wouldn't listen. Now we must account for his blood!'" (vv. 21-22).

Hearing his brothers' regret was almost more than Joseph could bear, and he was forced to hide his face from them so they wouldn't see the tears streaming down his cheeks. Before sending them back to Canaan, he ordered his servants to return their money secretly to their bags, along with the grain they'd purchased.

When the brothers realized what had been done, they reacted with fear:

> "[One of them] said to his brothers, 'My money has been returned! It's here in my bag.' Their hearts sank. Trembling, they turned to one another and said, 'What is this that God has done to us?'" (v. 28).

When the brothers returned home, Jacob was more than reluctant to send Benjamin with them back to Egypt. Rachel had passed away by that time, and Jacob was terrified of losing the only remaining child of his beloved wife.

Surprisingly, it was Judah—the same brother who planned to murder Joseph—who changed Jacob's mind by offering to be his brother's keeper:

> "Then Judah said to his father Israel, 'Send the boy with me. We will be on our way so that we may live and not die—neither we, nor you, nor our children. I will be responsible for him. You can hold me personally accountable! If I do not bring him back to you and set him before you, I will be guilty before you forever'" (Genesis 43:8-9).

Back in Egypt, Joseph ordered that a feast be prepared at his home in order to honor his brothers. Once again, they reacted with fear and couldn't receive the good offered to them. Joseph was again overcome with emotion at the sight of his brothers—especially of Benjamin, his mother's son. He had to run into another room in order to weep without being seen.

As his brothers prepared to journey back to Canaan once again, Joseph set his final plan in motion. His steward hid Joseph's favorite goblet in Benjamin's bag. Then, when the brothers were a little ways from the palace, Joseph sent the steward with guards to accuse them of stealing. Convinced of their innocence, the brothers allowed the steward to search their bags—they even promised that if anything was found they would all stay in Egypt as slaves and the thief would be punished by death.

Imagine their horror when the steward opened Benjamin's bag and pulled out the cup.

The guards brought everyone back to Joseph, and he gave this judgment: 11 of the brothers could return home, but Benjamin had to remain in Egypt as his slave.

This was the crucial moment. More than 20 years ago, these same brothers had sold Joseph as a slave because he was their father's favorite. Now they were being given a chance to get rid of another favorite son, and they didn't even have to lift a finger.

 "Then the Lord said to Cain, 'Where is your brother Abel?' 'I don't know,' he replied. 'Am I my brother's guardian?'" (Genesis 4:9).

Once again, it was Judah who stepped forward to speak:

> "Your servant became accountable to my father for the boy, saying, 'If I do
> not return him to you, I will always bear the guilt for sinning against you,
> my father.' Now please let your servant remain here as my lord's slave, in
> place of the boy. Let him go back with his brothers. For how can I go back
> to my father without the boy? I could not bear to see the grief that would
> overwhelm my father" (Genesis 44:32-34).

It was a big step. The same brother who was willing to trade Joseph's life for a little cash was
now desperate to trade his own life for Benjamin's.

Joseph lost control of his emotions once again—the text tells us he wept so loudly that
even those in the hallways could hear him. Finally, he revealed himself to his brothers. They
were terrified, of course, and Joseph had to work hard to convince them that he meant
them no harm. Eventually, they all had a warm, joyful reunion.

But the story didn't end there. Joseph sent his brothers home to fetch their father and bring
all of their families and possessions back to Egypt. And we expect a joyful response once
they arrive. Finally, Jacob would know that his son was alive!

What actually happened was a little anti-climactic:

> "So they went up from Egypt and came to their father Jacob in the land of
> Canaan. They said, 'Joseph is still alive, and he is ruler over all the land of
> Egypt!' Jacob was stunned, for he did not believe them. But when they told
> Jacob all that Joseph had said to them, and when he saw the wagons that
> Joseph had sent to transport him, the spirit of their father Jacob revived"
> (Genesis 45:25-27).

Jacob's first reaction was disbelief. He had to be convinced with evidence and arguments
before he would allow himself to think that something so good might be true.

What's your reaction to this chain of events?

**What's your opinion of Joseph's plan for testing his brothers? Was he right or wrong
to put them through it?**

Leading a group? It's the way to go.
Find extra questions and teaching
tools in the leader kit, available at
threadsmedia.com/creationrestored.

Lessons Learned

We process this complex web of events by focusing on each individual's reaction to the blessings set in front of him. Joseph, his brothers, and Jacob all responded to good news in drastically different ways.

Joseph could barely hold himself together. Seeing his brothers again and hearing that his father was alive and well brought him to tears. Seeing with his own eyes that his brothers' hearts had changed overtook him with emotion. His emotions were untempered and unrestrained; they burst out of him.

Joseph had allowed suffering to soften his heart, and his deep trust that God was working for him through his sufferings freed him up to receive blessings from God.

The opposite was true of Jacob. The disappointment of losing his favorite son had hardened him. His heart was frozen and numb to the point where he couldn't believe the news that his beloved son was alive and well.

Joseph's brothers responded to blessings with fear. Having committed a great evil against their brother, they were unable to feel gratitude when good things came their way in Egypt. They couldn't accept a good turn and receive it. They expected to be repaid with evil because of their sins, and so they were afraid.

What are the best things in your life right now?

How do you respond to those blessings? With fear like Joseph's brothers? With a hard, unbelieving heart like Jacob? Or with a full heart like Joseph?

Sometimes it's not the hard times that tear us away from dependence and trust in God. Some of us have learned to manage our storms, but we can't handle the sunny days. We understand that we don't deserve any blessings, and so we're suspicious when good things come our way.

Some of us experience emotionless prayers because we believe that God has already decided what He plans on doing anyway—and it probably won't be what we ask. When good things do happen, some of us wonder if we're being tested or if God is up to something with His "tricky kindness."

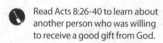

Read Acts 8:26-40 to learn about another person who was willing to receive a good gift from God.

Only with a right view of God's goodness and sovereignty will we be able to respond to God's good gifts with a free heart.

If we don't understand Him, we'll fear the blessings in our lives or doubt that such blessings are even possible. When we understand His kind, sovereign rule in our lives, we'll be blessed with tender hearts. We'll be able to experience hope without the fear of disappointment. We'll be able to receive good things from God without apathy or fear.

FREE TO FORGIVE

Jacob did travel to Egypt, bringing all the members of his household and all of their possessions. Pharaoh granted him the land of Goshen, where his family settled down and thrived. Jacob saw Joseph again and blessed his son—he was even able to bless his grandsons. And then, after a long and fruitful life, he passed away.

The death of their father made Joseph's brothers very aware of their dependence on Joseph, and very nervous that he might choose to retract his earlier forgiveness now that his father wasn't around to see it.

> "When Joseph's brothers saw that their father was dead, they said to one another, 'If Joseph is holding a grudge against us, he will certainly repay us for all the suffering we caused him.'
>
> "So they sent this message to Joseph, 'Before he died your father gave a command: "Say this to Joseph: Please forgive your brothers' transgression and their sin—the suffering they caused you." Therefore, please forgive the transgression of the servants of the God of your father.' Joseph wept when their message came to him. Then his brothers also came to him, bowed down before him, and said, 'We are your slaves!'" (Genesis 50:15-18).

The brothers were still afraid. They were still unable to wrap their minds around the idea that Joseph had forgiven them—really and truly forgiven them—for all the suffering he experienced at their hands.

For his part, Joseph did his best to explain that his forgiveness was genuine:

> "But Joseph said to them, 'Don't be afraid. Am I in the place of God? You planned evil against me; God planned it for good to bring about the present result—the survival of many people. Therefore don't be afraid. I will take care of you and your little ones.' And he comforted them and spoke kindly to them" (Genesis 50:19-21).

Joseph could forgive his brothers because he acknowledged that forgiveness ultimately belongs to God. In the same way that he knew committing adultery with Potiphar's wife would have been a sin against God, he knew that his brothers' attempt to kill him was also a sin against God. It was God's place to punish or forgive, not his.

Joseph's brothers could only see the consequences of their evil deed—all the ways their actions had cost Joseph. But Joseph saw everything that was accomplished for him and for God. He saw all the ways God was moving and working for the preservation of His people.

Joseph's forgiveness was more than a mere thought in his heart. More than a simple willingness to "let go of the past." Much more than our modern option of saying, "I'll forgive, but I won't forget."

Joseph's forgiveness was an active desire to seek his brothers' good. It wasn't just mercy; it was a pursuit, even at cost to himself, of his brothers' good.

That kind of forgiveness has several important characteristics.

Joseph's Forgiveness

First, Joseph's forgiveness wasn't conditional. He may have waited until he finally saw the change in his brothers' hearts to reveal who he was, but Joseph began blessing them long before that. Before he knew their hearts had changed, he wept twice. Before he knew they were genuinely different, he prepared a feast for them and filled their sacks with grain and money.

Second, his forgiveness didn't seek their shame. Joseph didn't want his brothers to feel angry with themselves or disturbed by what they'd done. He didn't forgive them in a self-righteous way in order to prove he was the bigger man. He wasn't interested in belittling his brothers or making them feel guilty. Instead, he longed for them to feel peace and relief.

Third, his forgiveness sought to bless them. Joseph didn't just restrain his anger against his brothers. He did more than part ways with them peacefully. He invited them into his life and spent all he'd been given in order to serve and provide for them.

Is it easy or hard for you to forgive those who have wronged you? Why?

Maybe you're thinking: *I wish I could experience that kind of forgiveness.* Here's some good news: You can. In fact, you may have experienced it already.

 "Forgiveness is the key which unlocks the door of resentment and the handcuffs of hatred. It breaks the chains of bitterness and the shackles of selfishness." —Corrie ten Boom[2]

SESSION SEVEN CREATION RESTORED

God's Forgiveness

Joseph's forgiveness for his brothers was actually a reflection of the way God chooses to forgive all His children—including us.

God's forgiveness is unconditional. While we were still sinners, while we were still far off, God ran out to meet us and offer us grace. He sought to bless us with the gracious sacrifice of Christ long before we were even alive to ask for that gift.

God's forgiveness doesn't seek our shame. God doesn't try to emotionally blackmail us into loving Him. He's not interested in belittling us or holding our failures over our heads. Instead, He took all of our shame and assigned it to His own Son—freeing us from the charges forever.

God's forgiveness seeks to bless us. His forgiveness didn't end with a peace treaty that would save us from death. He gave us far more. He's not only cleared our record, He's re-written it with all of Jesus' perfect actions. Not only are we spared from hell, we're given heaven to enjoy Him forever.

What emotions do you experience when you think about God's forgiveness?

Which element of God's forgiveness do you value most? Why?

AN AMAZING EPILOGUE

Near the end of Genesis, God spoke directly to a human for the first time in Joseph's lifetime:

> "That night God spoke to Israel in a vision: 'Jacob, Jacob!' He said. And Jacob replied, 'Here I am.'
>
> "God said, 'I am God, the God of your father. Do not be afraid to go down to Egypt, for I will make you into a great nation there. I will go down with you to Egypt, and I will also bring you back. Joseph will put his hands on your eyes'" (Genesis 46:2-4).

This is an amazing conversation. God had two motives in taking Jacob to Egypt: His glory and Jacob's good.

Listen to "Long Time Traveller" by The Wailin' Jennys from the *Creation Restored* playlist, available at *threadsmedia.com/creationrestored.*

As we discussed in session five, God had a big vision in mind for these events. He was taking Jacob into Egypt as a way of preserving His people. He was fulfilling the promises made to Abraham and Isaac. He was setting the stage for an exodus that would exalt His name so visibly that it couldn't be missed by anyone walking on the earth. But in the midst of that great plan, God did not let the tiny details of Jacob's life slip His mind. He wanted to give Jacob the kindness of a reunion with his beloved son before he died.

As followers of God, we have a tendency to emphasize one aspect of God's purposes. We sometimes fall into the trap of thinking that God doesn't care about the details—the tiny, passing moments that bring us joy each day. We think He doesn't remember or care that we want a spouse, a child, or one more moment with our loved ones. As a result, we feel foolish or selfish troubling Him with our requests. We assume He has bigger things on His mind.

At other times we focus on the details without remembering God's bigger picture. We know He cares about the little things, so we ask Him to help us find parking spots and give us more time to finish up a project at work. As a result, we lose sight of God's greatness and glory. We have a hard time caring about God's mission to reach all the nations, or the fact that His name is His greatest passion.

Think of Jacob and remember this: God is out for His glory and He's out for our good. Both are true. This passage reminds us that He is willing and able to accomplish both.

Which direction do you lean more often when it comes to God's purposes in your life? How can you tell?

Do you think there are prayer requests that are "too small" to bring to God? Why or why not?

Where does your life fit into God's bigger picture for the Church and the world?

Maybe hearing about Joseph and Jacob makes you sad because you don't see that kind of happy ending down the road in your life. Maybe you don't know how your story could possibly turn out for good. Maybe life is hard, and you're trying desperately to get your act together so God doesn't think you're self-obsessed and weak.

 "Aren't two sparrows sold for a penny? Yet not one of them falls to the ground without your Father's consent. But even the hairs of your head have all been counted. So don't be afraid therefore; you are worth more than many sparrows" (Matthew 10:29-31).

The good news—the gospel that can't be hidden in Genesis—is that God is for you. He cares about the large and small details of your story. He cares about your to-do list and the deep hurts and desires in your heart. He hasn't forgotten you, and He's not frustrated with you.

But also be comforted by the truth that bigger things are happening through you and around you. God is going to be exalted, and He's going to do it not in spite of your suffering, but through your suffering. Find comfort by zooming out and embracing God's great plan.

Joseph was faithful in the details of his own life, and through all his pain, God was at work to restore a family. He was at work to heal their sin and join them together. He was at work to restore Israel and to keep His promises to His people. Through Joseph's suffering, God was working out a plan to keep His people alive.

If we zoom out a little further, we can see a bigger pattern. We see a faithful Creator preparing the way for a great Savior who would rescue His people and provide for them in a way that puts Joseph to shame.

If we zoom out further still, we can see that God was at work through the suffering of Joseph to save two pastors in Texas who would be born thousands of years later. And He was working through Joseph's suffering to save you, too!

Do you believe that all of this is true? Why or why not?

THE END

We look at these stories in Genesis, and for a moment it all makes sense. For a moment, the clouds clear and we can see that God is doing everything for our good. For a moment, we can see His handprint on Abraham and Isaac and Jacob and Joseph.

But their lives seem miraculous. Their God seems miraculous. And at the end of the day, our lives and our perceptions of God feel bland and boring in comparison. Of course those guys could live for God. They met with Him. They talked with Him. They had His assurance of how the story was going to turn out.

Our stories seem a little more broken. Our lives a little messier. And we have no idea how our stories will end—or do we? The truth is, this story was written down for us so that we could live our lives in light of the end. The Book of Genesis was recorded so that we would know that the same God working things out for Jacob and Joseph is on His throne today, working things out for us.

Just as Joseph was given a vision of how it would all be in the end, so are we. God has recorded the end of the story for all of us who are in Christ:

> "Then I heard a loud voice from the throne:
>
> "Look! God's dwelling is with humanity, and He will live with them. They will be His people, and God Himself will be with them and be their God. He will wipe away every tear from their eyes. Death will no longer exist; grief, crying, and pain will exist no longer, because the previous things have passed away.
>
> "Then the One seated on the throne said, 'Look! I am making everything new.' He also said, 'Write, because these words are faithful and true.' And He said to me, 'It is done! I am the Alpha and the Omega, the Beginning and the End. I will give water as a gift to the thirsty from the spring of life. The victor will inherit these things, and I will be his God, and he will be My son'" (Revelation 21:3-7).

We know the end of our stories. The words above represent the trajectory of every soul who lives in Jesus. It ends with our exaltation in Christ. It ends with no more tears and no more pain. It ends with Jesus. It ends with the Alpha and the Omega being ours for eternity and us being His.

You're probably aware of that intellectually. But just stop for a second. Shut your eyes and imagine something with me: imagine you believe that it's true.

Imagine you believe the God of Abraham sits on His throne today. Imagine the God who wrestled with Jacob is living and active. Imagine the Father who steered Joseph's life is steering yours in the same way. Read the verses above one more time. Read them and imagine you believe that's really how this whole thing will wrap up.

Because it's true. Your story will end with a "happily ever after."

The gospel is true. That's why it's truly able to give you freedom.

APPLY TO LIFE

Carry a notebook around with you this week and write down any piece of good news that you receive—anything from someone complimenting your outfit to an announcement that you've won a prestigious award. At the end of the week, review your notes and answer the following questions:

1. What are your initial reactions when you look at the list?
2. What about the list is most surprising?
3. What is your favorite piece of good news? Why?

To commemorate the end of this study, read Genesis 1 and Revelation 22 in the same sitting. What kinds of connections do you see between the two texts?

Now that you've experienced "The Gospel According to Genesis," make a commitment to share what you've learned. Pray throughout this week that the Holy Spirit will give you an opportunity to share the gospel of Jesus Christ with someone who needs it. (And when the opportunity comes, be sure to take advantage of your chance.)

END NOTES

SESSION 1
1. Walter Brueggeman, *Genesis* (Louisville, KY: John Knox, 1982), 116-117.
2. Tim Keller, *What Were We Put in the World to Do?* (New York: Redeemer Presbyterian Church, 2006), 94.
3. Ligon Duncan, "The Promises of God," January 3, 1999 [Cited 5 January 2012]. Available from the Internet: *www.fpcjackson.org*.
4. John Piper, "The Faith of Noah, Abraham, and Sarah," June 22, 1997 [Cited 5 January 2012]. Available from the Internet: *www.desiringgod.org*.
5. A. W. Tozer, *The Knowledge of the Holy* (New York: Harper Collins, 1961), 62.

SESSION 2
1. Tim Keller, *What Were We Put in the World to Do?*, 153.
2. J. C. Ryle, *Holiness* (LaVergne, TN: Lightning Source, 2001), 95.
3. The Barna Group, "Research on How God Transforms Lives Reveals a 10-Stop Journey," March 17, 2011 [Cited 30 January 2012]. Available from the Internet: *www.barna.org*.

SESSION 3
1. Charles Spurgeon, *Morning and Evening,* rev. ed. (New Kensington, PA: Whitaker House, 2001), 673.
2. Gretchen Livingston and Kim Parker, "A Tale of Two Fathers," June 15, 2011 [Cited 30 January 2012]. Available from the Internet: *www.pewresearch.org*.

SESSION 4
1. Gilbert Thomas, William Cowper and the Eighteenth Century (London: Ivor Nocholson and Watson, Ltd., 1935), 132.
2. PewResearchCenter Publications, "Americans and Social Trust: Who, Where, and Why," February 22, 2007 [Cited 30 January 2012]. Available from the Internet: *www.pewresearch.org*.

SESSION 5
1. C. S. Lewis, *The Problem of Pain* (New York: HarperCollins, 1996), 91.

SESSION 6

1. Blaise Pascal, *Pensees* (Boston: MobileReference, 2010), 546.
2. The Barna Group, "Teenagers Want Succesful Careers and Global Travel, Expect to Delay Marriage and Parenting," May 10, 2010 [Cited 30 January 2012]. Available from the Internet: *www.barna.org*.

SESSION 7

1. PewResearchCenter Publications, "Morality of Premarital Sex," March 14, 2007 [Cited 31 January 2012]. Available from the Internet: *www.pewresearch.org*.
2. Corrie Ten Boom, *Tramp for the Lord* (Fort Washington, PA: CLC Publications, 2008), 197.

Threads

An advocate of churches and people like you, Threads provides Bible studies and events designed to:

cultivate community We need people we can call when the tire's flat or when we get the promotion. And it's those people—the day-in-day-out people—who we want to walk through life with and learn about God from.

provide depth Kiddie pools are for kids. We're looking to dive in, head first, to all the hard-to-talk-about topics, tough questions, and thought-provoking Scriptures. We think this is a good thing, because we're in process. We're becoming. And who we're becoming isn't shallow.

lift up responsibility We are committed to being responsible—doing the right things like recycling and volunteering. And we're also trying to grow in our understanding of what it means to share the gospel, serve the poor, love our neighbors, tithe, and make wise choices about our time, money, and relationships.

encourage connection We're looking for connection with our church, our community, with somebody who's willing to walk along side us and give us a little advice here and there. We'd like opportunities to pour our lives out for others because we're willing to do that walk-along-side thing for someone else, too. We have a lot to learn from people older and younger than us. From the body of Christ.

We're glad you picked up this study. Please come by and visit us at *threadsmedia.com*.

ALSO FROM THREADS . . .

CREATION UNRAVELED
THE GOSPEL ACCORDING TO GENESIS
BY MATT CARTER AND HALIM SUH

The words we read in Genesis are the same words that provided hope for hungry Israelites in the wilderness, breathed courage into the heart of David, and fed the soul of Jesus Himself during His time on earth. God's promises are as relevant today as they were "in the beginning."

Matt Carter serves as lead pastor of The Austin Stone Community Church in Austin, Texas. He and his wife, Jennifer, have three children.

Halim Suh and his wife, Angela, also have three kids. Halim is an elder and pastor of equipping at The Austin Stone Community Church.

SEVEN DAILY SINS
HOW THE GOSPEL REDEEMS OUR DEEPEST DESIRES
BY JARED C. WILSON

The words we read in Genesis are the same words that provided hope for hungry Israelites in the wilderness, breathed courage into the heart of David, and fed the soul of Jesus Himself during His time on earth. God's promises are as relevant today as they were "in the beginning."

Jared C. Wilson is the author of several books, including Gospel Wakefulness *and* Your Jesus Is Too Safe: Outgrowing a Drive-Thru, Feel-Good Savior. *He is the pastor of Middletown Church in Middletown Springs, Vermont. Visit him online at jaredcwilson.com.*

MENTOR
HOW ALONG-THE-WAY DISCIPLESHIP WILL CHANGE YOUR LIFE
BY CHUCK LAWLESS

Drawing from biblical examples like Jesus and His disciples and Paul and Timothy, author Chuck Lawless explores the life-transforming process of a mentoring relationship. This study is both a practical and spiritual guide to biblical mentoring, providing easy-to-model life application for how to have and be a mentor.

Chuck Lawless is vice president for Global Theological Advance of the International Mission Board. The author of several books, Dr. Lawless is also president of the Lawless Group, a church consulting firm (thelawlessgroup.com).